ATTENTION WITHOUT TENSION

A TEACHER'S HANDBOOK ON ATTENTION DISORDERS
(ADHD AND ADD)

Edna D. Copeland, Ph.D.
Valerie L. Love, M.Ed.

Specialty Press, Inc.
Plantation, Florida
1995

Copeland, Edna D. and Love, Valerie L.
    Attention Without Tension: A Teacher's Handbook on
    Attention Disorders (ADHD and ADD)
    p. 175

    ISBN 1-886941-01-7   (pbk.)

    1. Attention Deficit Disorder - Treatment
    2. Attention-deficit/Hyperactivity Disorder - Treatment

Specialty Press, Inc.   • First edition 1995
300 Northwest 70th Avenue
Plantation, Florida 33317
(800) 233-9273 • (305) 792-8101

Manufactured in the United States of America

ACKNOWLEDGMENTS

We are grateful to all the teachers and parents who have shared their success stories with us and encouraged us to prepare this handbook; to the children with attention disorders who have come into our lives and given us an understanding of their struggles and challenges; to Terry Love for his creative cartoons; and to Ron Walker for his contributions to classroom management strategies.

ATTENTION WITHOUT TENSION

A Teacher's Handbook on Attention Disorders

(ADHD and ADD)

TABLE OF CONTENTS

Introduction   1

UNDERSTANDING ATTENTION DISORDERS

1. Key Facts About Children With Attention Disorders   4
2. What are Attention Disorders?   5
3. History of ADHD   7
4. Reluctance to Identify ADHD   8
5. Legal Issues and Legal Rights of ADHD Students   10
6. Validity of ADHD Syndrome   14
7. Causes of ADHD   17
8. Learning Disabilities and Attention Disorders   21
9. Language Disorders, Reading Disorders and
    ADHD in Preschoolers   23
10. Learning Style Preference and ADHD   24
11. Developmental Readiness and ADHD   26
12. Characteristics of Children With ADHD   30

TREATING ATTENTION DISORDERS

13. Developing an Action Plan   38
14. Roles of the Members of the Treatment Team   46
15. Psychological/Psychoeducational Evaluation   57
16. Treatment Approaches   74
    A. Medication   74
    B. Behavior Management Strategies   80
    C. Psychological Interventions   88
    D. Educational Intervention   91

MANAGING ATTENTION DISORDERS

17. Statement of Objectives   93
18. Managing ADHD in the Classroom   96

        A. General Strategies   96
        B. Specific Strategies   102

19. Teacher's Success Story   112
20. References   114

SUPPLEMENTAL MATERIALS

21. Appendix of Forms   118

IDENTIFICATION AND GOAL SETTING

 1. Problem solving assessment   119
 2. My student's behavior   120
 3. Child/adolescent's assessment of home/school   121
 4. Overall summary for meeting with child/parents   123
 5. Two-week goals   124
 6. Academic summary   125
 7. Letter to parents   126
 8. Letter to professional   127
 9. Written consent   128
10. *Preschool Check Up: A Symptom Checklist for
     Developmental Disabilities*   129
11. *A Check-Up for Elementary School Children*   131
12. *A Checkup for Adolescents: A Symptom Checklist
     for Behavioral, Attentional, Learning and Emotional
     Difficulties*   133
13. *Copeland Symptom Checklist For Attention
     Deficit Disorders*   135
14. *Copeland Symptom Checklist for Adult Attention
     Deficit Disorders*   137
15. Scoring the *Copeland Symptom Checklists*   139

MEDICATION

16. *Medication Schedule*   141
17. *Medication Weekly Record Form*   142
18. *Copeland Medication Follow-Up Questionnaire*   143
19. *Medication - Side Effects Check List*   144

RESPONSIBILITY PROGRAMS

20. Responsibility chart (elementary children)   145
21. Chipper Bear responsibility chart (preschoolers)   146
22. Responsibility chart (teenagers)   147
23. Family organization calendar   148

CLASSROOM MANAGEMENT AND ORGANIZATION

(Scheduling)

24. Sample daily schedule   150
25. Daily assignment sheet   151

(Homework)

26. Elementary school weekly homework sheet   152
27. Middle/high school weekly homework sheet   153
28. Daily homework sheet   154
29. Daily class, homework and test record   155

(Writing paper)

30. Graph paper for math - 1" squares   156
31. Graph paper - 3/4" squares   157
32. Graph paper - 1/2" squares   158
33. Small graph paper - 1/4" squares   159

(Progress reports)

34. Daily progress report (older student example)   160
35. Daily progress report (older student form)   161
36. Daily progress report (younger student example)   162
37. Daily progress report (younger student form)   163

RESOURCE MATERIAL

38. National support groups and associations   165
39. U.S. Department of Education Clarification of Policy   166
40. List of regional Civil Rights Offices   172
41. Suggested readings and audioprograms for
    parents, teachers and professionals   173

INTRODUCTION

Teaching can be, and has traditionally been, one of the most rewarding professions. It is the means by which our values, beliefs, heritage and accumulated knowledge are transmitted to future generations. It is, perhaps, a way of ensuring some sense of our own immortality.

Teaching, however, is not always easy. Even under ideal conditions it can be exhausting, and frustrating moments are inevitable. It does not pay nearly enough to compensate for the demands of the job. Neither the pay nor its status in our country acknowledges the fundamental role teachers play in the long-term welfare of our nation. Teaching as a *profession* is only beginning to be recognized.

Despite these obstacles, you have, for some reason, chosen to teach. Perhaps, in your childhood a teacher's belief in you made that special difference. You, in turn, may hope to contribute to making the school experience for the children of this generation a positive one. You may have chosen this profession because you have a genuine compassion and fondness for children. The intangible rewards to be obtained from helping a child to understand himself and his world a little better are more important to you than the satisfaction of other endeavors. Those special moments when a child masters something he could not do before, or when you provide the encouragement to help a child succeed may make it all worthwhile. Perhaps you know that if one child fails, we have all failed. Whatever your reasons, you persevere. We are grateful for your choice and encourage you to continue your efforts to make a difference.

As a teacher, you have immense influence and possess tremendous power in the lives of children. They admire and respect you and have faith that what you tell them is true. You unknowingly, and often unwittingly, shape and mold their lives in thousands of large and small ways, many of which are not fully realized for years to come. You have the opportunity to help create an adult who will be a confident, capable, contributing member of society. Guiding and nurturing a young mind is perhaps your ultimate reward as a teacher.

Of all the tools at your disposal, none is greater than your ability to influence a child's self-esteem. Research has shown continuously that what a child believes about himself he will become. If *you* believe that a child has potential and promise, *he* will believe it, too. As you recognize and encourage his unique talents and traits, he believes himself to be valuable and special. One study of hyperactive children who became successful adults revealed that the major factor contributing to their positive outcome was having one person in their childhood who believed in them. Often this person was a caring and concerned teacher.

2

It is not always easy, however, to believe in a child and see his positive traits, especially if he has an attention disorder. It can be difficult to remain positive when he disrupts your class, loses papers, irritates fellow classmates and seems bent upon defying you at every turn. The paradox is, however, that these challenging and demanding children need your support and encouragement more than others. Experience has shown that these highly energetic and creative children often become successful entrepreneurs and business executives--*if* they survive the school experience! Your belief in them at an early age can be instrumental in guiding them through the often rough seas of childhood and adolescence.

We are delighted to assist you with this endeavor. It is our hope that this handbook will make your job a little easier and a lot more rewarding. We applaud you as you undertake man's most important challenge . . . that of raising our children.

"Physicians, lawyers, and architects can leave visible and lasting records of their important contributions to their professions and society: a pioneering new treatment or surgical procedure, a precedent-setting judicial decision, a soaring skyscraper. The contribution of the teacher is not so breathtaking. It is intangible, immeasurable, invisible--given to children, one by one. But, as most of us can attest, the teacher's contribution influences us for a lifetime. And in so doing, as Henry Adams said, it 'affects eternity'." Ronald A. Wolk, Teacher Magazine, April, 1990

UNDERSTANDING ATTENTION DISORDERS

KEY FACTS ABOUT CHILDREN/ADOLESCENTS WITH ATTENTION DISORDERS

APPROXIMATELY 3 TO 6% OF CHILDREN ARE AFFECTED.

- ADHD, Hyperactive-Impulsive and Combined Type   2 - 4%
- ADHD, Inattentive Type   4 - 6%

THEY MAKE UP 30 TO 40% OF ALL REFERRALS TO CHILD PSYCHOLOGISTS, PSYCHIATRISTS AND MENTAL HEALTH AGENCIES

BOYS OUTNUMBER GIRLS FROM 2:1 TO 4:1.

- Boys show more aggression, loss of control and inappropriate acting-out behavior.

- Girls are significantly underidentified.

- Girls have more language and cognitive deficits, underachievement, depression and social problems.

WHEN UNIDENTIFIED AND UNTREATED, ADHD/ADD CHILDREN ARE AT MUCH GREATER RISK FOR:

- Academic underachievement

- School failure and dropout

- Drug and alcohol abuse

- Teen pregnancy

- Emotional problems

- Social problems

- Legal problems

- Auto accidents

- Economic underachievement as adults

WHAT ARE ATTENTION DISORDERS?

There are approximately forty-five million children in the United States under the age of eighteen. It is conservatively estimated that three to six percent of them have an attention disorder, a neurobiologic condition characterized by the inability to pay attention and impulsiveness. Some are overactive, others are merely restless, and still others are sluggish and underactive. Attention disorders occur in people of every ability level and in every socioeconomic group throughout the world. They are believed to occur more frequently in boys than in girls.

Attentional problems usually begin in early childhood or in the elementary school years. They often continue into adolescence and adulthood and can last a lifetime. They can be difficult to recognize, for the symptoms often appear to be learning disabilities, emotional problems, bad behavior, poor parenting, stressed-out environments, and overly demanding schools, among others.

Each child or adolescent with an attention disorder manifests the difficulties in a unique and individual way. Much scientific research has, therefore, been conducted in an attempt to identify and define the central problem. ADHD has existed for hundreds of years and has been known by different names including *Minimal Brain Damage, Minimal Brain Dysfunction (MBD), Hyperkinetic Reaction of Childhood, Attention Deficit Disorder With and Without Hyperactivity, Attention Deficit Hyperactivity Disorder (ADHD) and Undifferentiated Attention Deficit Disorder* (UADD).

The current diagnostic criteria for Attention-Deficit/Hyperactivity Disorder have been established by the 1994 *American Psychiatric Association Diagnostic and Statistical Manual of Mental Disorders (DSM-IV^TM)*. Three categories are outlined:

- *Attention-Deficit/Hyperactivity Disorder, Predominantly Inattentive Type.*
- *Attention-Deficit/Hyperactivity Disorder, Hyperactive-Impulsive Type.*
- *Attention-Deficit/Hyperactivity Disorder, Combined Type.*

There is growing concern among experts in the field that there are many more children, adolescents and adults affected by *ADHD, Inattentive Type* than previously thought. There are also far more girls and women with this type than with the *Hyperactive/Impulsive Type.*

"A child's spirit is like a child, you can never catch it by running after it; you must stand still, and, for love, it will soon itself come back." Arthur Miller, THE CRUCIBLE 1953

DIAGNOSTIC CRITERIA FOR
ATTENTION-DEFICIT/HYPERACTIVITY DISORDER[1]

Either (1) or (2)

   (1)   six (or more) of the following symptoms of <u>inattention</u> have persisted for at least 6 months to a degree that is maladaptive and inconsistent with developmental level:

INATTENTION

   (a)   often fails to give close attention to details or makes careless mistakes in schoolwork, work, or other activities

   (b)   often has difficulty sustaining attention in tasks or play activities

   (c)   often does not seem to listen when spoken to directly

   (d)   often does not follow through on instructions and fails to finish schoolwork, chores, or duties in the workplace (not due to oppositional behavior or failure to understand instructions)

   (e)   often has difficulty organizing tasks and activities

   (f)   often avoids, dislikes, or is reluctant to engage in tasks that require sustained mental effort (such as schoolwork or homework)

   (g)   often loses things necessary for tasks or activities (e.g., toys, school assignments, pencils, books, or tools)

   (h)   is often easily distracted by extraneous stimuli

   (i)   is often forgetful in daily activities

   (2)   *six (or more) of the following symptoms of <u>hyperactivity-impulsivity</u> have persisted for at least 6 months to a degree that is maladaptive and inconsistent with developmental level:*

HYPERACTIVITY

   (a)   often fidgets with hands or feet or squirms in seat

   (b)   often leaves seat in classroom or in other situations in which remaining seated is expected

   (c)   often runs about or climbs excessively in situations in which it is inappropriate (in adolescents or adults, may be limited to subjective feelings of restlessness)

   (d)   often has difficulty playing or engaging in leisure activities quietly

   (e)   is often "on the go" or often acts as if "driven by a motor"

   (f)   often talks excessively

IMPULSIVITY

   (g)   often blurts out answers before questions have been completed

   (h)   often has difficulty awaiting turn

   (i)   often interrupts or intrudes on others (e.g., butts into conversations or games)

[1]Reprinted with permission from the *Diagnostic and Statistical Manual of Mental Disorders, Fourth Edition.* Copyright 1994, American Psychiatric Association

A BRIEF HISTORY OF ATTENTION DISORDERS

1800's	*Fidgety Phil* - A character in stories written by a German family doctor for his children.
1902	George Still, M.D. - *Lancet* - Description of ADD - still valid in the 1990's.
1940's	Outbreak of encephalitis. Symptoms were similar to those of hyperactive children. Therefore, deduced that hyperactive children were brain damaged.
1960's	Decided hyperactive children were not brain damaged. Name changed to *Minimal Brain Dysfunction (MBD)*.
1965	Diagnostic category established by American Psychiatric Association: *Hyperkinetic Reaction of Childhood*. Hyperactivity was defined, not as a biological problem, but, an environmental one.
1965-1980	Little information or accurate diagnosis. Mothers blamed for problems.
1980	*Attention Deficit Disorder With and Without Hyperactivity* diagnosis established by the American Psychiatric Association. Primary problems: poor attention, impulsivity and overactivity.
1987	Name changed again to *Attention-deficit Hyperactivity Disorder (ADHD)* and *Undifferentiated Attention Deficit Disorder*.
1994	Diagnosis of ADHD expanded to: *ADHD, Predominantly Inattentive Type; ADHD, Predominantly Hyperactive-Impulsive Type; and ADHD, Combined Type*.

Note

For purposes of simplicity, we shall use the term *ADHD* throughout this handbook to represent all types of attention disorders. To avoid the cumbersome repetition of two pronouns, we shall use the term *he* to refer to all students with attention problems; *she* to refer to all teachers; and *he* to refer to all physicians. The words *child* and *children* will be used to refer to all students from preschool age through adolescence.

THE RELUCTANCE TO IDENTIFY:

WHY OUR SYSTEM FAILS OUR CHILDREN

For many, many children who are referred for a psychological evaluation in elementary and even in high school for learning, behavioral and/or emotional problems, one has only to look at early school records or talk with their teachers to realize that most children with problems experienced difficulties early in their school lives. Had these early *warnings* been identified as the symptoms they would become, and had they been addressed, these problems would probably have been resolved successfully.

RELUCTANCE

Teachers, however, are frequently reluctant to identify a child as "suspect" for learning, attending or emotional problems. They often prefer to cope rather than to call for help. Nevertheless, educators must take on this responsibility, for they are usually the first to observe the problem. Their judgments are also usually quite accurate. Research has, in fact, consistently shown that teachers' assessments are remarkably similar to those of psychologists, psychiatrists and learning specialists in identifying the child who needs special help. Reluctance to say a child has problems is the first deterrent to early identification and helpful intervention.

VALUE OF PRIVACY

A second deterrent to identifying children with problems is the high, often impregnable fortress of personal privacy we believe people to have, i.e., the right and privilege of a person and family in a free society to mind their own business and have others mind theirs. For this reason, teachers may hesitate to discuss with parents a student's behaviors that appear unusual or inappropriate for his age. Nevertheless, if prevention of emotional, attending and learning disorders is to take place, the intervention must take place before the problems are severe, ideally at the first sign of difficulty.

BELIEF IT WILL PASS

A third deterrent is our hope that it is only a stage--that the child will *grow out of it*. Unfortunately, however, many children go through years of anguish while parents, teachers and others await the magic moment. For many, that day never comes, but rather the day that things are so bad that there is no recourse. The child now has a *bona fide* problem and must receive attention.

EMPHASIS ON SOLUTIONS

A fourth problem is our American tradition of *curing* problems after they exist instead of *preventing* them. We see this approach in every area of our lives--in our economy, our environment, our energy resources, medicine, education and certainly in mental health.

FEAR OF UPSETTING PARENTS

A fifth problem is our fear of telling parents and causing emotional turmoil. Teachers are basically caring people or they would not be in this field. They do not like to hurt or anger parents. And yet teachers must be prepared to deal with every gamut of emotional response from intense anger to deep despair to guilt. People do respond emotionally when confronted with a reality they have not recognized, that they have denied, or that they have prayed would *go away* with the magic of growth.

FEAR OF LITIGATION

The final factor is the current litigious climate in which all of us live. Teachers have been instructed in many school districts *not* to identify problems. The intent, we truly believe, was to avoid the problem of teachers making a medical *diagnosis*. However, teachers and schools have a responsibility to note behaviors and learning difficulties and to bring these to the attention of parents. Lawsuits for *omission* of this duty have been filed in some states. The solution appears to be in identifying and alerting parents to difficulties, yet avoiding diagnosing; to refrain from making specific treatment recommendations, especially those involving medication; and to establish a positive, collaborative relationship among all those who will be involved in helping the child.

We encourage you to become knowledgeable and to share your concerns with parents and professionals. Your intervention may well determine your students' success or failure . . . not only in school but in life.

LEGAL ISSUES AND LEGAL RIGHTS

OF ADHD STUDENTS

Attention disorders represent a relatively new field of educational awareness, and over the past several years have become increasingly controversial in terms of understanding the level of service and responsibility that state and local educational agencies play in addressing the needs of the ADHD/ADD child or adolescent. Two federal statutes are revelant to understanding the legal rights of ADHD/ADD students within the schools: the Individuals with Disabilities Education Act (IDEA), originally formulated in 1975 as the Education of the Handicapped Act (EHA), and Section 504 of Public Law 93-112, the Rehabilitation Act of 1973. A recent clarification by the Federal Department of Education issued in September of 1991 detailed the particular services and level of responsibility that school districts must provide under IDEA while issues of accommodation under Section 504 continue to evolve and develop.

INDIVIDUALS WITH DISABILITIES EDUCATION ACT
(FORMERLY THE EDUCATION OF THE HANDICAPPED ACT)

IDEA guarantees special education services to children and adolescents who qualify for service under a variety of handicapping conditions, including learning disabilities, behavior disorders, and emotional handicaps. Specifically included in the original legislation was a category labeled "Other Health Impaired" (OHI) which formerly had been used primarily to classify students with neurologic and physical impairments such as cerebral palsy, muscular sclerosis and epilepsy. In the recent clarification memo, however, the Department of Education specifically ruled that ADHD/ADD is a handicapping condition under IDEA, specifically referring to its inclusion as a neurological/medical condition under OHI.

The recent research detailing the biochemical and neurological bases of attention disorders has almost certainly played a pivotal role in this policy of change. Previously, many ADHD students did not qualify for specialized services within the schools. Research indicates that probably no more than 20-30% of them have qualified in varying school districts because of discrepancy formulas which required significant differences between measurements of intellect and ability. Particularly at early ages, before the attentional problems had a chance to significantly impact academic performance, many ADHD students have not qualified for service, although increasing numbers of them do qualify at later ages as the cumulative school effects become more pronounced. This diagnostic model is ill-suited to serving effectively ADHD/ ADD students in the schools since it is corrective rather than preventative in nature, and research strongly indicates that early intervention and preventive measures are most effective in addressing the needs of ADHD individuals.

In the current formulation, ADHD is a diagnosable handicapping condition under Federal Special Education laws, utilizing the OHI classification, if the condition is "chronic and acute," resulting in "limited alertness," which "significantly adversely affects educational performance." In some respects this new wording is less than helpful to individual school districts since the terms "limited alertness" themselves are not defined. Many ADHD students do not show limited alertness *per se*, but limited alertness only specific to the relevant information in the classroom. In fact, they may be quite alert to external stimuli and information irrelevant to the learning process, but not alert at all to the teacher's instructions, written work or tests. As a result, at this point, it remains uncertain what percentage of children with ADHD may qualify for special education services, and almost certainly individual school districts will draw up widely varying policies regarding this matter. Nevertheless, the clarification does represent a landmark change in policy such that school districts clearly must establish a specific manner of deciding which ADHD children do qualify for special education specifically on the basis of that handicapping condition and find appropriate ways to address these problems.

In addition, the clarification of IDEA also restates the testing requirements specific to all handicapping conditions. Many districts have previously adopted policies in which parents were told that the school district could not, or did not, assess for attention disorders, since ADHD was not a handicapping condition under P.L. 94-142. The clarification memo states quite bluntly that any condition which is handicappable under IDEA does require testing. It additionally restates that this testing must be done in a timely manner, that is, sixty days from the date of parent request to the determination of eligibility. While the federal government has provided no additional funds to comply with this memorandum, it is easy to see that significantly increased burdens for both testing and specialized services could conceivably be placed on local school districts. Other areas of concern are that current psychological and testing services in many districts are grossly overloaded and could hardly begin to serve all of the ADHD children who might need to be tested, and that the staff in these services, while competent, have often not been specifically trained to assess attention disorders. Conflict between the assessment of a medical condition through the utilization of psychometric tests by school personnel often not trained in the disorder is another issue which will gradually be resolved through school policy and undoubtedly through some litigation procedures over the next several years.

As special education law currently stands, students with attention disorders do qualify for special education services, at least in some cases where their condition appears to be relatively severe and persistent. Many more students with ADHD, however, qualify for evaluation and testing, since testing services are available "regardless of the severity of the handicap," and at parental request only. While the degree of services that the law insists must be provided by state and local school agencies has broadened considerably over the last several years, specific plans of action or funding for such increased entitlements have not been forthcoming at the federal level. As a consequence, many state and local school districts are likely to be caught between the increasing demands of parents for services consistent with their children's rights under federal law, and pragmatic considerations that necessary money and staff are not available to provide all the services which are necessary.

SECTION 504, PUBLIC LAW 93-112

Prior to the clarification memo, an increasing number of parents sought services for their ADHD students in the schools through utilization of Section 504 of Public Law 93-112. This law, the Rehabilitation Act of 1973, was not originally intended as education law, but it does define a handicapped individual as anyone who experiences a "mental, psychological or physiologic disorder which interferes with an individual's civil right to one or more major life activities." The list of major life activities which is included in the law includes "learning," and therefore expands the definition of handicapping condition specific to the classroom environment. The primary difference between IDEA and Section 504 is that Section 504 provisions extend to the regular classroom, as well as special education classes, and it is not necessary that the child qualify for special education services to be subject to the provisions of Section 504. Indeed, a host of cases have now held that any modifications which can be made in the regular education classroom appropriate to a child's difficulties or handicaps must be made.

Section 504 is administered through the Office of Civil Rights, and parent complaints under Section 504 are initially reviewed by OCR and then arbitrated by an *impartial adjudicator*, who can be selected neither by the parents nor by the school itself, and must be agreed upon by both parties. Hundreds of these arbitration proceedings have now been conducted in regard to ADHD and the schools, and a standard of *minimal accommodation* is increasingly apparent. Essentially the standard which has been set in OCR complaints is that if the parent can document either through testing by the school or outside professionals, or by samples of student work and teacher reports that the child has difficulties—mental, psychological or physiologic— which interfere with his ability to learn in the classroom, that the classroom teacher and school must make whatever accommodations can be ruled to be appropriate so long as these accommodations are not unduly expensive and do not interfere with the learning of others. An example of the minimal accommodation standard for students who have difficulty taking notes or copying from the board has been that arbitration rulings have held that it is not necessary for the school district to provide a paraprofessional as a full-time notetaker for the child, but that it is necessary that the school district require a teacher to make a precopied set of the notes, or assign another student who is a good notetaker, to copy his notes, so that the student with the notetaking handicap is not unduly penalized for his condition.

In a number of other areas regarding specific difficulties students have in the classroom, but which would not be qualifiable under IDEA, the arbitration proceedings have reached similar rulings such that it is incumbent upon the school district and regular education teachers to modify classroom curricula and procedures to whatever extent possible without impairing the education of other students in the classroom. The developing standards under Section 504 are not yet fixed, but it is clear that the Section 504 criteria apply specifically to ADHD students, and that school districts will have to make modifications, even in the regular classroom, for ADHD students who do not qualify for special education assistance. A list of possible accommodations, which is taken directly from arbitration proceedings and civil litigation regarding Section 504, is included toward the end of the clarification memo, which also stresses school districts' responsibilities in regular education programs to ADHD students.

SUMMARY

The scope of legal responsibilities in the schools to ADHD students is greatly expanding. Consistent with other areas of federal policy change, such as the inclusion of ADHD/ADD as a handicapping condition under Federal Social Security Administration laws and Medicaid reimbursement, the courts and the Office of Civil Rights have increasingly held that such students must be provided services which are appropriate to their educational and behavioral needs. Some ADHD students, and possibly an increased number of them, will qualify for services under special education law. Of more critical importance to schools, however, is the understanding that these students qualify for specialized service and accommodation within the regular classroom even if they do not qualify under special education law. It is clear that the field of legal responsibilities of the schools to these students is hardly finalized, and that close attention should be paid by school officials to the ongoing establishment of legal criteria for ADHD students under both IDEA and Section 504 of P.L. 93-112.

For the interested reader, a full copy of the memorandum is available in the Appendix.

VALIDITY OF ADHD SYNDROME

The validity of the concept of attention deficit disorders, both with and without hyperactivity, has periodically been the subject of questioning and controversy. It is, therefore, important to review some of the history concerning this issue.

In 1970, *The Myth of the Hyperactive Child* was written in response to increased use of stimulant medication in California. This book created fear and uncertainty in the minds of many and is believed to have delayed the investigation and treatment of this disorder for many years. While the book received widespread attention, the Congressional investigation in 1971 which resulted from the controversy it generated was hardly noticed. It is significant, however, that the report stated:

> In summary, there is a place for stimulant medications in the treatment of the hyperkinetic behavioral disturbance, but these medications are not the only form of effective treatment. We recommend a code of ethical practices in the promotion of medicines, and candor, meticulous care and restraint on the part of the media, professionals and the public. Expanded programs of continuing education for those concerned with the health care of the young, and also sustained research into their problems, are urgently needed.

It further stated:

> Our society is facing a crisis in its competence and willingness to develop and deliver authentic knowledge about complex problems. Without such knowledge, the public cannot be protected against half-truths and sensationalism, nor can the public advance its concern for the health of children.

In the mid- to late 1980's, a group antagonistic to psychiatry supported litigation in several states whereby parents filed lawsuits against school boards, physicians, the American Psychiatric Association, principals and teachers, among others. This group sensationalized ADHD, especially the use of medications such as Ritalin in the treatment of it. Widespread media attention was subsequently given to attention deficit disorders, especially to the use of stimulant medication. Most of the publicity was quite negative.

Again, these complaints led to an investigation by Congress. The Secretary of Health and Human Services convened an interagency committee of the National Institutes of Health to report to Congress on learning disabilities. The Committee concluded that:

Pharmacotherapy for ADD originated 50 years ago, and at the present time the ameliorative effects of medications in ADD are well established. Despite concerns in the early 1970s that medications, primarily stimulants, were being prescribed too frequently, recent data and the experience of most clinicians indicate that this is not the case. The general skepticism of experienced clinicians, coupled with a climate where parents are reluctant to medicate children, serves to limit their use except where indicated.

It also recommended a greater research focus on defining characteristics of the whole spectrum of ADD patients, noting that currently "the number of affected children may be seriously underestimated".

Ciba-Geigy Pharmaceutical Company, the manufacturer of Ritalin, was investigated that same spring of 1988 by the FDA. The investigative report stated: "We have completed our review of your report, as well as other materials, and are reassured that information accumulated since the approval of Ritalin provides additional support for its efficacy and safety in use under the conditions of use recommended in its currently approved labeling."

Despite continued investigation and documentation by the best minds in the field, some continued to question whether "hyperactivity . . . is really a disorder at all." Alfie Kohn, in a scholarly report in *The Atlantic Monthly* (November 1989), researched the field as the skilled reporter he is and raised disturbing questions. His criticisms appear more accurately addressed to diagnostic and treatment methodologies than to the construct itself. Nevertheless, the article was summarized without critique and reprinted in *Education Week* (November 22, 1989). Those with only a cursory knowledge of the field are, therefore, left somewhat confused and uncertain. Parents are often especially troubled by such controversy. Professionals and teachers must deal with their anxiety and misinformation on a daily basis.

While ADHD and ADD have experienced some of the same validation problems inherent in other medical disorders which have many possible origins, including ear infections, hypertension, migraine headaches and hydrocephalus, most investigators accept and support the concept of ADHD.

The neurobiological nature of attention disorders has been the subject of much research investigation. In a recent landmark study reported in *The New England Journal of Medicine* (1990), Dr. Alan Zametkin and his associates at the National Institute of Mental Health found that hyperactive adults who have been hyperactive since childhood, and who also have hyperactive children, had decreased glucose metabolism rates in the prefrontal cortex and the premotor cortex, as well as a more global decreased rate of glucose metabolism. They found differences in the metabolic rate of other regions of the brain as well.

The findings of Dr. Zametkin and his associates, while still somewhat preliminary, have forever, hopefully, established ADHD as a neurobiological disorder and not a myth or an excuse for poor parenting or teaching.

It is important that educators, and professionals be comfortable with the validity of the concept of attention deficit disorder, for they will, in all likelihood, be exposed periodically to controversy surrounding it. Part of your job will be educating parents to help them overcome their misinformation and anxiety about ADHD. As a teacher, you are encouraged to review all points of view. Encourage parents to do the same. Only then can one be satisfied that one's knowledge and actions are consistent with the truth, as best it can be known at any given moment, and ultimately with one's goals for the ADHD child whom you teach.

"The one real object of education is to leave a man in the condition of continually asking questions."
Bishop Creighton, Quoted C. A. Alington, THINGS ANCIENT AND MODERN

CAUSES OF ATTENTION DISORDERS

ADHD is a complicated problem and, like other physiological problems, has multiple causes. At this time, most researchers and practitioners consider accurately diagnosed attention disorders to be physiological problems and *not* behavioral, emotional, learning or environmental problems. New techniques for studying the brain offer great hope for further understanding. Computerized brain scans (BEAMS), blood flow studies, Magnetic Resonance Imaging (MRI), and Positron Emission Tomography (PET) will contribute significantly to our growing body of knowledge about ADHD and ADD.

Causes of attention disorders are grouped into five major categories:

1) *Constitutional or innate biological factors.* These relate particularly to temperament and heredity.
2) *Organic factors.* Organic factors include all physiological insults and injury to the central nervous system and/or brain.
3) *Diet, nutrition, allergies, and food intolerances.*
4) *Environmental toxins, including lead, formaldehyde and chemical pesticides, among others.*
5) *Attention disorders secondary to other medical problems.*

Social, cultural, educational, and stress factors can cause or exacerbate attentional problems in many children and adolescents.

While scientific knowledge is very incomplete in this area, attention deficit disorders are considered neurophysiological problems resulting from variations from the norm in brain chemistry. These differences may be genetic or they may be the result of problems in the development of the child before birth. Some attention deficit disorders result from infection or trauma after birth. These problems are usually more difficult to treat than inherited ADHD/ADD, usually involving some degree of brain injury. Environmental toxins, especially lead and some chemicals used in pesticides, are known to cause ADHD symptoms. Drugs and/or alcohol ingested during pregnancy can cause severe ADHD and learning problems. ADHD is sometimes considered a temperamental variation to the extreme.

The preponderance of research in this area strongly suggests that the majority of attention disorders, regardless of cause, result from a deficiency or imbalance of neurotransmitters or brain chemicals. These brain chemicals affect the frontal and central brain structures important for alertness and attention, and the premotor cortex responsible for motor inhibition and impulse control.

To understand ADHD, one must understand the structure of the brain. The following discussion is simplified and represents the most generally accepted view of the neurophysiology of attention deficit disorders today. As our knowledge increases, our understanding will become both increasingly accurate and more complex.

Neurotransmission

The brain consists of billions of neurons, or nerve cells, the basic structure of the brain. Information is processed through a complex process of electrical and chemical transmission. For example, when a stimulus, such as an external noise or an internal thought, impinges on the brain at a level strong enough to reach excitatory potential, the neuron fires and a nerve impulse is conveyed from the nucleus of the nerve body out the length of the axon to varying numbers of dendrites of other cells. To pass to another cell, the nerve signal must cross a tiny gap called a *synaptic cleft* or *synapse.*

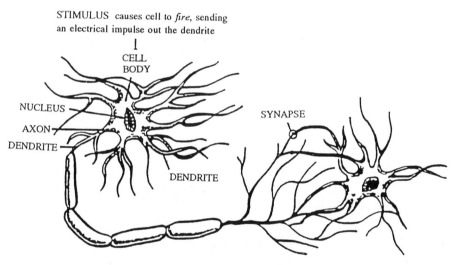

STIMULUS causes cell to *fire,* sending
an electrical impulse out the dendrite

CELL BODY

NUCLEUS

AXON

DENDRITE

DENDRITE

SYNAPSE

TWO NEURONS IN SYNAPTIC CONTACT

At the synapse, the *electrical* signal releases a chemical called a *neurotransmitter* which is stored in vesicles, or packets, on the *presynaptic dendrite.* Once the neurotransmitter has been released and is absorbed by an appropriate receptor on the *post-synaptic dendrite,* the message continues its electrical transmission to the next synapse. It is the neurotransmitters which enable the electrical impulse to be transmitted from one dendrite to another. Without the neurotransmitters, the relay of impulses in the brain would be impossible.

19

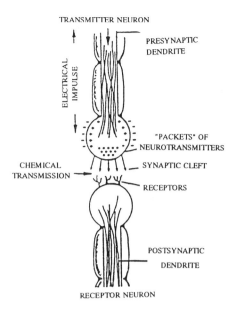

Many disorders are known to be the result of specific neurotransmitter deficiencies or excesses including Parkinson's Disease, Alzheimer's and Autism, for example. The neurotransmitters most frequently implicated by the research in ADHD/ADD are norepinephrine and dopamine, with dopamine currently considered the more important.

Neurotransmission is a complex process and involves both excitatory and inhibitory neurons. Inhibition is equally, if not more, important than excitation. In fact, the more sophisticated the organism, the more inhibitory neurons it has. Each physiological response is a complex interplay between all those inhibitory and excitatory neurons being stimulated and transmitting impulses at any given time.

Each neurotransmitter has a special function and each affects particular nerve cells in particular parts of the brain. ADHD and ADD have, for several years, been considered neurotransmitter disorders. Some medications used to treat attention disorders increase the availability of the neurotransmitters on the presynaptic dendrites (Ritalin and Dexedrine, for example), while others prevent the re-uptake of the neurotransmitters, leaving more available at the synaptic cleft (Norpramin and Tofranil, for example). The exact mechanisms of the medications traditionally used for ADHD and ADD are addressed at length in *Medications for Attention Disorders: (ADHD/ADD) and Related Medical Problems*.

Brain functioning is obviously a very complicated process with many potential sources of breakdown. Its complexity renders a search for easy solutions a futile endeavor. A comprehensive understanding of attention disorders is years away. A rudimentary knowledge of the brain does, at least, give us a roadmap. It helps us understand the effect of various interventions, both medical and nonmedical, and have greater confidence in the benefits of these treatments.

THE IMPORTANCE OF CORRECT DIAGNOSIS OF ADHD

While true attention deficit disorders are physiologically caused, there can be many difficulties that create ADHD-like behavior. These include: allergies, food intolerances, hypo- and hyperthyroidism, depression, manic-depressive illness, auditory processing problems, learning disabilities, poor parenting, disorganized environments, and excessive stress, among others. For example,

- ADHD is often improperly diagnosed as an educational problem and tutoring or remediation is recommended. While additional educational assistance in a one-on-one or small group situation is helpful, it does not address the root problem and will not produce lasting benefits.

  - If ADHD is misdiagnosed as a learning disability, the student will be given much tutoring and remediation but will continue to fall further and further behind because the attention problems interfere so drastically with efficient learning.

  - ADHD is frequently misdiagnosed as a family problem--one that is caused by ineffective parenting or parental conflict. Mothers are blamed for lack of discipline, while fathers are faulted for lack of time and presumably lack of interest. Psychotherapy or insight into the family interaction problems may provide some relief, but rarely do they significantly affect the problem. Both parents, child and therapist are often frustrated by the slow progress made or the lack of progress altogether.

  - If allergies are incorrectly diagnosed as ADHD and are treated with stimulant medication, the child is likely to get worse, although some children do improve to some degree.

  - If an anxious child is misdiagnosed as having ADHD and is given stimulant medication, he is likely to be even more teary, agitated and labile. On the other hand, an ADHD child who is misdiagnosed as anxious and treated with play therapy will have a wonderful time but is not likely to improve either at home or at school.

  - The symptoms of hyperthyroidism, which include rapid heart beat, irritability, and over-reactivity, will be intensified by stimulant medication. It is critical to rule out any other medical causes of the ADHD symptoms.

  - Children and adolescents who will later develop manic-depressive illness often present as overactive children. While some respond positively to stimulant medication, others will experience the greatest relief of symptoms if treated with lithium.

From these descriptions, it is clear that a correct diagnosis of the student's problems is crucial. If not, intervention is likely to be both inappropriate and ineffective. For this reason, referral to a professional is often recommended.

LEARNING DISABILITIES AND ATTENTION DISORDERS

ADHD is considered by some to be a learning disability. However, most professionals in the field view the two as separate, although frequently related, difficulties. In 1987, the Interagency Committee on Learning Disabilities recommended in its report to Congress that a new definition of learning disabilities be adopted. The modified definition is as follows (changes to previous definition underlined):

"Learning disabilities is a generic term that refers to a heterogeneous group of disorders manifested by significant difficulties in the acquisition and use of listening, speaking, reading, writing, reasoning or mathematical abilities, or of social skills. These disorders are intrinsic to the individual and presumed to be due to central nervous **system** dysfunction. Even though a learning disability may occur concomitantly with other handicapping conditions (e.g., sensory impairment, mental retardation, social and emotional disturbance), with socioenvironmental influences (e.g., cultural differences, insufficient or inappropriate instruction, psychogenic factors) and especially with attention deficit disorder, all of which may cause learning problems, a learning disability is not the direct result of those conditions or influences."

While most ADHD children do not have coexisting learning disabilities, eighty percent of them do have great difficulty with handwriting and do work that is described as *messy* or *sloppy*. ADHD children frequently perform poorly because they can either write quickly (producing *messy* work) or write neatly (taking four to five times longer than the average child) but cannot do both. "Quality versus quantity" becomes a major issue. For that twenty to forty percent who do have a coexisting learning disability, it is frequently one or more of the following:

- Auditory perception and processing problems
- Visual perception and visual processing problems
- Auditory and visual memory problems (both short- and long-term)
- Sequencing problems
- Fine-motor problems
- Visual-motor integration delays
- Poor eye-hand coordination and dysgraphia
- Dyslexia and reading disorders

- Written language problems

- Spelling disorders

- Math disorders

While intelligence is not affected *per se* by attention disorders, development of the intellect may be uneven, causing a child not to reach his potential. Usually by third grade I.Q. scores have dropped significantly, at which time the child's performance is often below his own ability level and that of the class. Low achievement test scores in areas requiring sustained effort and attention frequently result in the child being diagnosed as having learning disabilities when, in fact, he does not have learning disabilities but rather a long-standing, undiagnosed attention disorder. Having worked with both learning disabled and attention deficit youngsters for many years, we are convinced that at least fifty percent of those diagnosed as learning disabled are ADHD or ADD children who are underachieving so dramatically that they appear to have learning disabilities.

WITH YOUR GOOD EYE-HAND CO-ORDINATION, AND MY GOOD VERBAL SKILLS, WE MAKE A GREAT TEAM, ROGER.

"There is no surer way of calling the worst out of anyone than that of taking their worst as being their true selves; no surer way of bringing out the best than by only accepting that as being true of them."
E. F. Benson, REX

LANGUAGE DISORDERS, READING DISORDERS

AND ADHD IN PRESCHOOLERS

The implications of ADHD in language and reading disorders has received increasing attention as it becomes apparent that attentional deficits affect the preschooler's selective and sustained attention to the language he hears. Since 1985, the link between early oral language skills and reading has been clearly demonstrated, as well as the interaction of language, memory and attention on later reading ability. K. G. Butler, for example, tested 229 kindergarten children and followed them to the eleventh grade. Of the screening tests used, morphology, syntax, and attention were the most predictive of subsequent reading ability. Attention alone showed a high correlation with reading success.

Those of us who have worked with these children for many years have increasingly believed that inappropriate attending to language input and decreased ability to *lock* language into long-term memory have resulted in many auditory/language-based learning disorders. Increasingly research is supporting this point of view. It is believed that more than 50 percent of language-based learning disorders have their origins in poor attentional abilities in the early years. It is important that we identify those children with ADHD in the preschool years and effectively intervene in the attention disorder. While medication is often not an option because of the child's young age, dietary and allergic intervention, training in listening skills, increased attention to language development, behavior management programs, and specific speech and language therapy can prevent the disabling effect of ADHD on later reading and academic proficiency.

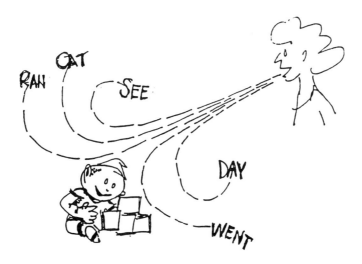

LEARNING STYLE PREFERENCE AND

ATTENTION DISORDERS

Exciting new research in the field of learning has revealed that brain dominance dramatically affects a person's approach to all areas of learning and living. Just as most people have a preference for right-handedness or left-handedness, most people are more comfortable operating out of either the right or left side of their brains. This brain dominance in many ways affects one's personality, language, problem-solving strategies, learning, organizational skills, approach to information, and emotions.

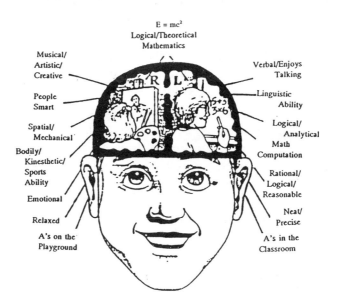

The left-brain child is analytical, sequential, explicit and concrete. His life is sensible, organized and on schedule. He has good verbal skills, is articulate, and goal-oriented. His desk, locker, notebook and papers will typically be organized, neat and completed on schedule. His style fits well with the expectations in most classrooms and causes both teachers and parents to be delighted with his academic progress.

Right-brain children, by contrast, tend to be intuitive, spontaneous, visual, playful, artistic, creative, nonverbal, emotional, and diffuse. The right side of the brain has been described as the side which keeps life disorganized, fun and off schedule. It is imaginative, fantasy-oriented, and random in its thinking processes. This child's locker and desk will, more often than not, be messy, overflowing and chaotic. It is frequently very hard to distinguish whether a child has attention problems or is just extremely right-brain. Children who are very right-brain are sometimes mistakenly diagnosed as having ADHD.

Attention problems, however, are found in both left and right-dominant children. In our experience, left-brain ADHD children have an easier time in school than right-brain ADHD children, who experience disorganization and lack of focus from both causes. Although a left-brain child with ADHD may be excessively tense and easily frustrated, he will typically focus much better than a right-brain ADHD child. With encouragement and guidance, left-brain ADHD children can learn to harness their abundance of energy and overactivity into outstanding productivity and accomplishment. Their analytic skills, organization, internal structure, and goal orientation often offset the poor focus, distractibility and impulsivity of the ADHD. The right brain ADHD child requires different teaching strategies in addition to treating the ADHD. With appropriate instruction and emphasis on their strengths, however, these creative children can become equally productive.

THE IMPORTANCE OF FIT

Sometimes the opposite natures of the child and the teacher will make the problems much more difficult. A very neat, left-brain teacher, for example, will have more difficulty tolerating a laid-back, disorganized, unruly ADHD child than will an easy-going, casual teacher. There is no right or wrong way for the teacher or the child to be. *Psychological fit*, however, can make a drastic difference in how a child and a teacher get along.

DEVELOPMENTAL READINESS AND

ATTENTION DISORDERS

Developmental readiness for the three R's of school is an important issue for all children and an especially crucial one for students who have attentional problems, whether on the daydreaming, underactive end of the continuum or the more restless, distractible, overactive end. Being age five does not guarantee success in kindergarten, nor does being age six assure success in first grade. To be successful, a student must be developmentally, *not chronologically*, mature. Immaturity is as much a handicap, both aca-demically and socially, for the third, eighth or eleventh grade student as it was in earlier years. Children who enter a particular grade before they are developmentally ready to cope with it are destined for failure. Strong academic skills, good achievement test scores, and above average intelligence help, but they do not guarantee success for the immature child. The ability to concentrate, to control one's impulses and to act appropriately are critical ingredients for academic accomplishment. Developmental maturity in the areas of auditory and visual processing, short- and long-term auditory and visual memory, sequencing, visual-motor integration, and fine- and gross-motor skills are also necessary components for success. Those students with even moderate delays can be expected to experience academic, social and emotional difficulties in school. Those who have difficulty in the classroom are likely to experience problems for the rest of their lives. In the classroom, as in life, success begets success, while failure only compounds itself.

A number of recent statistics underscore our need for careful assessment of a student's readiness for kindergarten and first grade as well as the appropriateness of his developmental placement for all grades:

Approximately 27 percent of our preschool and school-age children have developmental delays which range from mild to severe.

25 percent of all children who enter first grade will be behind by at least one grade level or will have repeated a grade by the fifth grade.

75 percent of all children referred to child developmental agencies, psychologists and psychiatrists are overplaced in school.

Summer Children (those whose 6th birthday occurs in June, July, August or later before they enter first grade):

- are less able to achieve academically at the level of their ability.

- suffer significant esteem problems in their elementary, junior and high school years.

- achieve less success and happiness in life.

- have more learning and emotional difficulties than any other age group.

- may have a considerably higher rate of suicide in adolescence.

Other data which indicate our need for careful assessment of readiness are:

At least two million children will be in Learning Disabilities programs next year. More than 500,000 will be in self-contained Behavior Disorders classes.

More than one million children will be on stimulant medication for attention deficit disorders. Some of these children will be hyperactive; others will not. All will have problems with attention, concentration and impulse control.

Many students diagnosed as having learning disabilities, behavior disorders, and attention deficit disorders are children who were simply not ready for the demands of today's accelerated academic programs. As a result, they have been unnecessarily diverted into learning disability and behavior disorders placements but frequently continue to have significant difficulty. The large number of children requiring stimulant medication probably includes many who are overplaced in school. We know, for example, that there is a direct correlation between a child's age and the ability to concentrate. Young children are neurologically less mature and far more easily distracted than their older classmates.

DETERMINING DEVELOPMENTAL READINESS

While many and varied factors contribute to poor academic performance and emotional problems in students, not enough weight has been given to genetic and age-related factors in many children with learning difficulties. These factors include:

1) The child's age at school entrance.

2) The child's sex.

3) His rate of neurological maturation, which, in turn, affects auditory and visual processing, fine- and gross-motor control, organization and attention.

4) Verbal facility (being left-brain vs. right-brain). We know that schools are predominantly left brain, that is, oriented to language, analytical thinking and logic. Because of this, left-brain children have an easier time in school than do right-brain children, especially after second grade.

5) Innate intelligence.

6) Neurologically determined attention, concentration and impulse control.

The presence of one or more of these variables on the negative side usually requires the child to repeat one or two grades so that his developmental age is similar to that of his peers during the school day. Without doing so, failure is a certainty. By doing so, one is more certain that the child's basic needs of love, security, recognition, and a sense of success and achievement can be met in the classroom.

As teachers and parents, we must stop children from failing in school. The place to start is before they enter first grade. Sometimes, however, parents and teachers adopt a "let's wait and see how the child does" attitude with the option of retention later on. Research and the opinions of parents and children stress that this is *not* a positive option. Getting off to a bad start can continue to cause problems even when the child is retained.

29

Huff, for example, studied a group of second graders in Ohio. He found that those children who were developmentally or chronologically young and for whom school entrance was delayed had a cumulative grade equivalent of second grade-sixth month at the beginning of second grade, while the early starters had a grade equivalent of second grade-first month. In addition, and very importantly, fifteen of the twenty-one early starters had been retained at least once. Thus, the younger group had been in school five months longer only to have achievement scores five months lower.

Thus, it is critical to make the right decision *before* the child enters kindergarten and first grade. The option of retention at a later date only partially makes up for the damage. It is apparent that the loss of esteem, the sense of failure, and the months of frustration continue to sap the child's later ability to cope with school.

One thing which should be emphasized, however, is that delaying school entrance or retaining a child should *not* be an alternative to diagnosing and treating learning disabilities, attention deficit disorders, and behavioral, medical or dietary problems which are present. A year of maturation certainly helps these difficulties but it does *not* make them go away. They should be addressed at the earliest possible moment so that a year of readiness or repetition does not merely put the child *on-hold* for a year. If an additional year is needed, the child should be evaluated so that his specific weaknesses can receive attention and his strengths can be maximized.

"Education bewildered me with knowledge and facts in which I was only mildly interested." Charles Chaplin, MY AUTOBIOGRAPHY, 1964

CHARACTERISTICS OF CHILDREN

WITH ATTENTION DISORDERS

Each child with ADHD or ADD has a unique set of symptoms and characteristics. This handbook is intended to assist you in recognizing the symptoms of attention disorders in your students. After understanding the difficulties associated with ADHD, you should be able to recognize the symptoms. If you do suspect that a student has ADHD, we urge you to encourage his family to seek professional assistance from someone thoroughly familiar with this disorder. Proper diagnosis is crucial to establishing appropriate and effective treatment interventions.

The major symptoms of ADHD originally described by the American Psychiatric Association and ones which continue to be viewed as major problems are divided into three categories. These are: (1) inattention and distractibility, (2) impulsivity, and (3) problems with activity level - either overactivity or underactivity.

INATTENTION/DISTRACTIBILITY

Almost every student with ADHD displays poor attention. It can be seen as a short attention span, inattentiveness, or an inability to concentrate. The student may miss important parts of directions or have difficulty staying on task. Spaciness, another quality of inattentiveness, is the inability of a child to notice important stimuli to which he should respond. For example, the student may have every intention of listening to the directions for the math homework. He does listen, but does not hear that it was to be done in pencil and not pen.

Another attention problem seen frequently in ADHD students is their choice of the wrong stimuli to which to respond. This student may be able to describe in detail the floral print on the teacher's dress, but she did not hear what the history homework is.

Distractibility is defined as becoming sidetracked by other stimuli which are not relevant to the task at hand. Distractions may be internal (such as the feelings of hunger) or external (the car outside, the pencil on the floor or the pictures on the wall).

The student's physiological inability to concentrate may also make it especially difficult for him to complete long tasks or ones he considers boring. His constant off-task behaviors and his avoiding settling down to work are frustrating for the teacher and student alike. As much as he wants to be successful in school, the ADHD child's physical limitations often cause him to be extremely disappointed in himself.

Indications of inattention and distractibility are:

- Short attention span
- Difficulty completing tasks
- Daydreaming
- Easily distracted
- Nicknames such as: "spacey," "dreamer"
- Much activity but little accomplishment
- Enthusiastic beginnings but poor endings

IMPULSIVITY

The inability to think before acting and to tolerate delay is considered by many to be the most serious and enduring problem for ADHD adolescents and adults. These children are usually not malicious--simply unthinking. Pulling Susie's pigtails, grabbing John's book, or speaking out in class often happen quickly and without negative intent. These students are also frequently disorganized and forgetful; they constantly lose assignments, books, papers or homework. Staying organized is perhaps the most difficult task for ADHD students, in spite of valiant attempts to *get it all together.*

Indications of impulsivity are:

- Excitability
- Low frustration tolerance
- Acting before thinking
- Disorganization
- Poor planning ability
- Excessive shifting from one activity to another
- Difficulty in group situations which require patience and taking turns
- Requiring much supervision
- Constantly in trouble for inappropriate behavior

ACTIVITY LEVEL PROBLEMS

Children with ADHD vary in their activity level, ranging from underactive and lethargic to overactive and hyperactive. *Not all children with attention disorders are hyperactive.* In fact, <u>most</u> are not. The underactive child, however, is often not recognized and, therefore, is least likely to receive help. He is generally not impulsive and does not display excessive motor activity. He does, however, have difficulty paying attention and may appear confused and depressed. He is often viewed as being *lazy, disinterested, or having a poor attitude.* Both parents and teachers are often frustrated with this student because of poor performance on all tasks requiring discipline, planning and organization.

The hyperactive child, by contrast, appears to be in constant motion. He may drum his fingers, interrupt in class, pick on his classmates or talk constantly. He has great difficulty sitting in his seat and often appears to be *nervous.* In unusual settings, or in a one-to-one situation, however, these students are frequently able to respond like other children at least for a while. Research has shown that the more restrictive the environment and the more concentration required, the more likely it is that restless and off-task behavior will occur.

Indications of activity level problems are:

Overactivity/Hyperactivity

- Restlessness -- either fidgetiness or being constantly on the go
- Diminished need for sleep
- Excessive talking
- Excessive running, jumping and climbing
- Motor restlessness during sleep; kicking covers off -- moving around constantly
- Difficulty staying seated at meals, in class, etc.; often walks around classroom

Underactivity

- Lethargy
- Daydreaming, spaciness
- Failure to complete tasks
- Inattention
- Poor leadership ability
- Difficulty in learning and performing

While the preceding characteristics of inattention, impulsivity and activity-level problems are the most common symptoms of ADHD, the following characteristics are also seen frequently in students with ADHD.

NONCOMPLIANCE

ADHD students frequently do not mind in class and do not behave in socially acceptable ways when relating to fellow classmates. Noncompliance is sometimes due to a lack of training in self-control and problem-solving. However, experts believe that, even with the best of training in these areas, some children will not develop these behaviors unless they are neurologically mature enough to acquire the language skills necessary to develop cognitive alternatives.

Indications of noncompliance are:

- Does not mind
- Is argumentative
- Disregards socially-accepted behavioral expectations
- *Forgets* -- more deeds of omission than commission

ATTENTION-GETTING BEHAVIOR

The ADHD child's need to be noticed at all times is perhaps the most frustrating characteristic for teachers to deal with in the classroom. His need for attention appears insatiable. He may blurt out questions, pick on the other children, use bad language or interrupt frequently. Under conditions of increased competition, attention-getting behavior accelerates even more. Just notice when the principal drops by!

Indications of attention-getting behavior are:

- Frequently needs to be the center of attention
- Constantly asks questions or interrupts
- Engages in bad language or negative behavior to gain attention
- Irritates and annoys siblings, peers and adults
- Is the *class clown*

IMMATURITY

Emotional, physical, neurological and social immaturity are typically present in the ADHD child. This becomes especially evident as expected tasks, such as learning cursive writing, for example, appear incredibly difficult for a student. These *late bloomers* may reach various levels of maturity six months to several years later than their classmates. For this reason, they frequently enjoy the company of younger classmates who are their neurological peers.

Indications of immaturity are:

- Much of the behavior is that of a younger child (responses are typical of children six months to two-plus years younger).
- Physical development is delayed; neurological development is delayed.
- Younger children are preferred and relationships are better.
- Emotional reactions are immature.

SCHOOL PROBLEMS

Poor school performance and underachievement are close to universal problems from preschool through college. An ADHD child usually has trouble because he cannot concentrate and complete the work. Learning that does not require concentration and disciplined effort, such as vocabulary, comprehension and general information, is less affected than academic tasks which require repetition, memory and problem-solving. The ADHD student's impaired ability to concentrate, to attend to what is said, and to lock information into long-term memory inhibit his acquisition of many academic skills and decrease his fund of knowledge.

Indications of school problems are:

- Underachievement in relation to ability is present (especially by third grade).
- Books, assignments, clothes and other material are lost.
- Auditory memory and auditory processing problems, or visual memory and visual processing problems are present.
- Learning disabilities may coexist with the ADHD.
- Handwriting is poor.
- Written work is often described as "messy" or "sloppy".

- Assignments are often not completed.
- Academic work is performed too quickly or too slowly.

EMOTIONAL DIFFICULTIES

The emotional problems experienced by many ADHD children may be the result of physiological or psychological causes. Their frequent irritability, moodiness and quick tempers can be constant challenges in the classroom. Ongoing underachievement, criticism, failure and frustration result in low self-esteem for the majority of ADHD children. Perceiving themselves as *dumb* or *different*, they all wish for someone or something to help them.

Indications of emotional difficulties are:

- Frequent and unpredictable mood swings: happy one minute and miserable the next; or good days and bad days
- Irritability
- Underreactive to pain/insensitive to danger
- Easily overstimulated; hard to stop once "revved up"
- Low frustration tolerance; excessive emotional reaction to frustrating situations
- Temper tantrums, angry outbursts
- Moodiness/lack of energy
- Low self-esteem

POOR PEER RELATIONS

Problems with peers often begin in preschool, especially for the hyperactive child. Aggression and teasing are seen most frequently in this age group, while bossiness, difficulty taking turns and impulsive acting-out cause problems in elementary and secondary school. ADD children who are not overactive often lack confidence and may develop only one or two best friends. Frequently on the fringe of their peer group, they often feel lonely and despondent.

Indications of poor peer relations are:

- Hits, bites, kicks and bosses other children
- Has difficulty following the rules of games and social interactions
- Is rejected or avoided by peers
- Is a loner and avoids group activities
- Teases peers and siblings excessively
- Bullies or bosses other children; wants to be the leader

FAMILY INTERACTION PROBLEMS

Attention disorders have a profound effect on the family, especially if the child is hyperactive. The activity level, constant difficulties, moodiness, and problems at school create much tension and anxiety for the parents and siblings of these children. The support and assistance of a knowledgeable, caring teacher can be invaluable to a family struggling with the problems of attention disorders.

Indications of family interaction problems are:

* There is frequent family conflict.
* Activities and social gatherings are unpleasant.
* Parents argue over discipline since nothing works.
* Mother spends hours and hours on homework with ADHD child leaving little time for others in family.
* Meals are frequently unpleasant.
* Arguments occur between parents and child over responsibilities and chores.
* Stress is continuous from child's social and academic problems.
* Parents, especially mother, feel:

___frustrated ___hopeless ___alone
___angry ___guilty ___afraid for child
___helpless ___disappointed ___sad and depressed

• • • • • • • • • • • • • • • • • • •

For a comprehensive list of the symptoms in each category, you are encouraged to review the Copeland Symptom Checklist for Attention Deficit Disorders included in the Appendix. As you will note, ADHD is differentiated from ADD. By completing the checklist, you can quickly assess areas of difficulty as well as areas of strength for a student suspected of having an Attention Disorder.

TREATING ATTENTION DISORDERS

DEVELOPING AN ACTION PLAN

It is often an alert, informed and caring teacher who first recognizes that a child is having difficulty. In your sincere desire to aid both this child and his family, you may be wondering whom to contact first and where to begin. Your role is a critical one in the life of your student at this point, for you may be instrumental in helping his family realize and understand the problems with which he is struggling. Your careful observation and reporting to the parents will give them the support they need to begin assembling a Team of professionals to assist their child.

It is virtually impossible for any one parent or professional to diagnose and manage attention disorders alone. Our experience has shown that those children who experience the most progress have an effective and caring Team behind them. This Team frequently includes not only the child, his parents and teacher, but also a number of other professionals such as a physician, psychologist, principal, tutor, psychiatrist, allergist, neurologist and other specialists. Your plans for managing and teaching this child in the classroom will be more successful if the parents are working with you at home and supporting your efforts. Our experience has shown the following ten-step plan to be the most efficient and effective way for a teacher to deal with a student she suspects may have ADHD.

TEACHER'S PLAN FOR SUCCESS

1) MEET WITH YOURSELF

You are encouraged to sit down, think through, define the immediate problems, and organize your strategy. You may even wish to start a folder labeled "(Student's Name): Strengths and Weaknesses." Make a list of all behaviors and academics that concern you and that are different from the majority of the other students. You may find the chart in the Appendix titled "Problem Solving Assessment" to be helpful. Note specific examples of each behavior, such as:

(1)   Poor Fine-Motor Coordination

     a. Can't tie shoelaces
     b. Difficulty in handwriting - large, messy, poor form

(2)   Poor Peer Relations

    a. Bosses other children
    b. Won't take turns
    c. Hits, shoves

If you have ways to verify these, do so. For example, if you suspect a memory problem, give the child three directions and see if he can follow them.

2) GATHER INFORMATION

Log the student's behaviors that occur over a 48-hour period. You may wish to use the chart in the Appendix entitled "My Student's Behavior." It is best to avoid trying to implement changes at this time. Try to analyze very objectively. Sometimes the problem is not the child, but the situation. For example, an overly *enriched* environment or an inappropriate placement in the classroom can make distractibility much worse. Lack of psychological fit between the student and teacher may be aggravating the problem.

3) ANALYZE INFORMATION

Next, you are encouraged to look at all the information you have on the child--test scores, psychological and medical reports, parents' comments, previous meetings, and past teachers' remarks. If the student attended your school last year, this is an excellent time to consult with that teacher. If you have guidance counselors or Special Education personnel, you may wish to consult with them and, if possible, ask them to observe the child in class.

4) MEET WITH THE STUDENT

Schedule a time to meet with the student. At that meeting, tell him you are concerned and are trying to understand him better. To do so, you need his input. Then discuss with him the items on the chart titled "Child/Adolescent's Assessment of Home and School" found in the Appendix. Explain to him that what he says is important and because you want to remember it, together you will record what he says. If either of you is uncomfortable writing it down, use the chart as a general outline to follow.

As you talk with him, try to reflect his feelings. Ask questions for understanding and clarification only. Try not to *judge* his response or change his perceptions, regardless of how you feel about what is being said. As your meeting progresses, try to organize problem areas. Have the child rank them in order of importance. Then discuss solutions he thinks would be helpful.

5) SET GOALS TOGETHER

After the problem areas have been discussed, decide upon some goals with your student. Let him know that you would like for the two of you to try to work it out first. Give your plan approximately one week, offering much support and encouragement for his efforts. If the problem areas continue, let him know that while he is trying, more help is needed. After the conference, complete the Symptom Checklist for Developmental Disabilities, the ADD Symptom Checklist and any other behavioral or learning checklists your school uses.

6) MEET WITH THE PARENTS

Phone the parents to schedule a conference and follow up with a letter which includes the checklists and information you wish them to complete before the conference. It is wise to include both parents, if possible, as this strengthens The Team. While ultimately parents will appreciate knowing about their child's problems, their initial reaction may seem negative. When a teacher points out a problem to parents, our experience has been that the reaction of some parents is fear, followed by anger, followed by defensiveness. On the other hand, some parents will experience a great sense of stress and anxiety about the child. And for still other parents, it may be a relief that someone else is also seeing the behavior in their child that they see at home.

As varied as parents' initial reactions may be, it is crucial that ultimately a positive collaborative relationship be established between teacher, parents and child. Everyone wants to be successful and everyone is trying to do a good job. When a child is not experiencing success in school, however, everyone feels threatened. It is easy for each person then to look for someone to blame. Parents may blame teachers, teachers may blame parents, and all inevitably blame the child. When both teachers and parents, however, are able to resist the temptation to become frustrated, the child has the strongest possibility of experiencing success. Only when home, school and professionals are all harmoniously working together can treatment be effective.

It is usually helpful to invite the principal, counselor or student support team from the school to join the conference. They have often observed the child and can be helpful in sharing their observations, both during the conference, and afterwards, as well.

DO'S AND DONT'S FOR A SUCCESSFUL PARENT CONFERENCE

DO . . Begin the conference by expressing your liking for the child and interest in him. Discuss his positive behaviors and strengths. Encourage the parents and child to share their opinions as well.

DO . . Address areas of concern, beginning with academic progress. Discuss problem areas, reviewing current grades or test scores. Review the Symptom Checklist and the ADD Symptom Checklists that both you and the parents have completed. They serve as an objective place to start and usually the forms completed by both are quite similar.

DO . . Be as specific as possible.

DON'T . . Attempt to diagnose. Children's behavioral difficulties are usually quite complicated. There are frequently many causative and contributing factors. ADHD is only one. Diagnosis is a complicated issue which usually involves a team of professionals. As a star member of The Team, your role in carefully observing and recording behaviors is crucial to help everyone involved ultimately understand the child.

DON'T . . Recommend Ritalin or any other medications for the child. Per-ceived pressure to give their children medication *to control behavior* has been at the heart of most of the lawsuits against and negative publicity toward schools. Medication issues must be determined by the physician involved.

7) ESTABLISH A TWO-WEEK STRATEGY

At the conclusion of the conference, you and the parents will want to decide upon a strategy to address specific target issues. This program should be implemented both at home and at school for two weeks. During this time there should be daily communication between parents and teachers. The methods employed will vary with each child, depending upon the problems defined. The strategies discussed in the Behavior Management section can be utilized as well as the organizational methods addressed.

MY TEACHER WILL BE OK
AS SOON AS SHE FINISHES
THIS BOOK.

43

8) MEET WITH PARENTS A SECOND TIME

After two weeks parents, teachers and child meet again. The severity of the problem and whether referral is indicated are usually apparent at this time. If the current strategy is working and the child has improved, the same program should be continued. Follow-up conferences should be scheduled as needed.

9) REFER PARENTS TO APPROPRIATE PROFESSIONALS

If the difficulties the child is encountering have not improved to a significant degree by the time of the second conference, in-depth assistance is usually required. Parents may wish to talk to the Special Education personnel (the Student Support Team, for example) at the school or consult with an outside professional.

The purpose of the Student Support Team (SST), often given a different name in each school, is to provide academic and behavioral intervention pro-grams for six to eight weeks before the family is referred to an outside professional or for a school-administered psychological/psychoeducational evaluation. If the child is having significant difficulty or if the child has ADHD, this additional time delay can be detrimental. Because of the tremendous work overload of special education in most schools and school districts, receiving meaningful assistance can take anywhere from two to ten months.

In our experience, a complete psychological/psychoeducational evaluation is almost always essential for every child who is having significant difficulty in school. Such an evaluation is important, for ADHD children often have coexisting learning problems, social problems and psychological problems which may mimic ADHD or may be caused by the attention disorder.

Because ADHD is a physiological problem and because it may resemble other medical problems, it is essential that a physician be involved in the evaluation of the student. Ideally the pediatrician or family physician should be involved even if a psychiatrist is also treating the child. A physical examination is recommended to rule out other medical possibilities. The child's physician or psychologist can make appropriate referrals to other professionals, based on the findings of clinical evaluations.

10) SHARE INFORMATION WITH PROFESSIONALS

To assist the professionals evaluating your student, it is important that you share with them your observations and concerns. The checklists you have completed on the student, the results of your two-week intervention program, and the evaluation forms you have completed with the parents and child may be very helpful to them. If not requested, you may wish to volunteer this information. Of course, you will need to obtain written permission from the parents. Your input is vital to the evaluation of the child, in assisting with treatment programs in the classroom, and in monitoring the effects of treatment.

If the professional involved is not knowledgeable about learning disabilities, developmental placement, learning-style preference, and other educational issues, it is especially important for you to bring these issues to the clinician's attention. Your comments and observations on the following issues, for example, may be crucial in assisting the clinician in formulating a diagnosis:

- Is the child not sufficiently challenged?

- Does the child have subtle learning disabilities in addition to the ADHD?

- Is the child overplaced? ADHD children are neurologically immature and are often not ready for the academic demands of their chronological peers.

- Does he have *learning gaps* created by his fluctuating attention span?

- Is the child a right-brain (visual/spatial) learner, or a left-brain (auditory/language) learner?

- Is placement in the gifted program helpful . . or is it creating additional and unnecessary stress?

Once the evaluation has been completed and a diagnosis has been made, a treatment program will be established. Your role will be a major one and will include: observing and recording the child's behaviors; implementing classroom recommendations; and maintaining regular contact with the other members of the Team.

"Human history becomes more and more a race between education and catastrophe." H. G. Wells, THE OUTLINE OF HISTORY 1920

ROLES OF THE MEMBERS OF THE

TREATMENT TEAM

TEACHER'S ROLE

1. Identify child/adolescent's problems/strengths at school

    a. Academic   b. Social/emotional/behavioral

2. Consult with child. Identify his sources of frustration and gratification. Enlist his thoughts about solutions.

3. Outline problem areas. Complete checklists:

    a. Academic
    b. Behavioral
    c. Attention and concentration (ADHD checklists)
    d. Learning strengths/weaknesses; brain dominance; CNS processing. (Symptom Checklist for Developmental Disabilities)

4. Meet with parents. Decide on problems, goals and strategies.

5. Implement two-week program at school that is coordinated at home. If significant problems continue,

6. Discuss with principal and/or other appropriate personnel.

7. Refer to Special Education and/or school counselor.

8. Complete information required by physician and other professionals. If not contacted, phone or write a letter indicating your interest and willingness to help.

9. Meet with professionals and parents and decide on strategy as a team.

10. Implement programs recommended at school.

11. Complete checklists on regular basis as agreed by the Team.

    a. Behavior charts
    b. Medicine Checklists (Benefits and Side Effects)

PARENT'S ROLE

1. Identify problems and strengths at home.

2. Consult with child. Identify his sources of frustration and gratification. Enlist his help in thinking of solutions.

3. Complete checklists and write down lists of:

    a. Academic strengths and weaknesses
    b. Behavioral strengths and weaknesses
    c. Child/adolescent's concerns about school
    d. Child/adolescent's concerns about home

4. Meet with teacher.

5. Implement two-week program at home. If significant problems are identified: refer to Special Education Services, the School Counselor, or

6. Consult a professional.

7. Educate yourself.

8. Seek out a support group.

9. Coordinate efforts of family, child, teachers and professionals.

10. Educate those important for your child's well-being.

11. Implement programs at home recommended by professionals.

CHILD/ADOLESCENT'S ROLE

1. Identify the problems as he perceives them at home and school.

2. Identify his strengths as he perceives them at home and school.

3. Identify his goals (realistic and *unrealistic*) at home and school.

4. Provide insight into why he's doing what he's doing:

    Ex. "Why hit Susie?" "Because she destroyed my room."
                                  "I'm ashamed of her."

    "Why not turn in homework?"   "Can't get organized - Just can't seem to keep it all together."

5. Offer possible solutions.

6. Help decide on plan of action.

7. Agree to try to implement the plan.

8. Help problem-solve when he cannot.

SCHOOL'S ROLE

1. Provide consultation and support to teacher.

2. Establish liaison between school, professional and parents.

3. Communicate interest in child and parents.

4. Help parents understand school's strengths and limitations in assisting w i t h problem.

5. When problems are identified:

    a. Refer to Special Education or Student Support Service
    b. Obtain psychological/psychoeducational evaluation
    c. Refer to school counselor
    d. Provide special education
    e. Assist parents in obtaining independent professional assistance (psychological, medical, and educational)
    f. Refer parents to support groups

    Where Available:

    a. Offer parenting groups for special needs
    b. Provide social skills training, esteem-building, and other counseling activities for child.

6. Provide educational information and resources to parents and teachers on:

    a. Learning disabilities and attention deficit disorders
    b. Behavior management strategies at home
    c. Classroom management strategies
    d. Discipline, responsibility and encouragement
    e. Self-esteem
    f. Brain dominance and learning style preference
    g. School readiness/overplacement in school

7. Provide seminars and training programs for parents, teachers and local professionals. Involve PTA/PTO.

PHYSICIAN'S ROLE

1. When appointment is scheduled for school-related problems, send appropriate questionnaires/checklists to be completed by parents and teachers before the appointment.

2. Meet with parents.

    a. Discuss concerns and review information.
    b. Obtain thorough medical history.
    c. Review developmental and school history.
    d. Review family, medical, learning and attending problems.

3. Meet with child/adolescent. Review concerns and solicit his views of problems at home and school. Informally assess his social/emotional status.

4. Give thorough physical examination

    a. Physical exam - include vision and hearing screening.
    b. Blood tests: Complete Chemical Profile, Thyroid Functioning Tests and Heavy Metals Testing, and others indicated.

5. As appropriate, refer to other professionals:

    a. Neurologist
    b. Ophthalmologist
    c. ENT Specialist
    d. Allergist
    e. Psychologist
    f. LD Specialist/Developmental Specialist/Speech and Language Pathologist
    g. Family Therapist/Social Worker
    h. Occupational Therapist or Physical Therapist

6. After diagnosis of ADHD:

    a. Educate parents on the range of treatment options available and help them decide which are most appropriate for their child and themselves.
    b. Begin treatment.
    c. Decide on Captain for the Team.
    d. Monitor your part of the treatment closely. Consult regularly with all other members of the team.

CHILD/ADOLESCENT

PSYCHOLOGIST'S ROLE

1. Evaluate child thoroughly:

    a. Psychological/emotional/esteem
    b. Intellectual strengths and weaknesses
    c. Educational

        1. Learning strengths and weaknesses
        2. Potential vs. achievement
        3. Learning disabilities

    d. Attention, concentration, impulse control
    e. Family relationships
    f. Peer/social relationships

2. Send findings to physician and school with parents' permission.

3. Confer with physician and teacher by phone or in person regarding the findings and recommendations.

4. Decide on roles of each *Team member* and who will be Captain. Determine with parent and other professionals who will be responsible for coordinating the Team efforts. Decide on and implement appropriate treatment plan.

5. Provide relevant and current educational information to parents and teachers on particular problems.

6. Provide psychotherapy/counseling to child and/or parent.

7. Offer or refer to a support group.

8. Refer to appropriate professionals for academic intervention, whether tutoring, LD remediation, family counseling, etc.

9. Be knowledgeable about special schools, legal issues, special education resources. Make specific recommendations.

10. Be actively involved in community education.

CHILD PSYCHIATRIST'S ROLE

1. Evaluate for ADHD. Differentiate from other psychiatric disorders, including conduct disorder, depression, manic-depressive illness, psychosis or pre-schizophrenia, among others.

2. Provide medical and psychological interventions for ADHD simultaneously.

3. Treat more severe emotional problems which may co-exist with ADHD.

4. Treat family members whose emotional problems are negatively impacting child, especially those requiring medical intervention as well as psychological.

5. Become "Captain of Team" when involved (usually).

6. Consult with teachers and school.

7. Provide group therapy experiences for parents and child.

8. Hospitalize child if necessary when problems are unmanageable or threatening to child's welfare or welfare of others.

9. Become actively involved in community education.

OTHER PROFESSIONALS' ROLES

NEUROLOGIST

1. Rule out seizure disorders, including complex partial seizures, narcolepsy, and others, as contributing factors. EEG and BEAM evaluations if indicated.

2. Monitor medication for seizures. May monitor medication for ADHD.

ALLERGIST

1. Determine presence of allergies, asthma and food intolerances.

2. Treat any problems found.

ENT SPECIALIST

1. Evaluate hearing and middle-ear fluid problems when child has history of chronic ear infections. Be aware of auditory processing problems and language-based learning disabilities sometimes resulting from chronic ear infections. Advise parents.

2. Assess presence of allergies. Evaluate or refer.

3. Treat any problems noted.

OPHTHALMOLOGIST

1. Evaluate vision and visual perception, depth perception, etc. thoroughly, especially when child presents with blurring words, slow copying from board, reading problems, family history of visual problems, clumsiness or poor coordination. Usually needed by second grade at latest.

2. Treat any visual problems diagnosed.

FAMILY THERAPIST/SOCIAL WORKER

1. Educate parents on ADHD and its effects on the family. Treat dysfunctional interactions in family.

2. Promote positive relationships and teach effective parenting interventions.

3. Provide psychotherapy for child and/or parents. Refer to appropriate professionals for specific interventions needed to promote overall family health: Support Groups, including Ch.A.D.D. (Children with Attention Deficit Disorders), ADDA (Attention Deficit Disorders Associations) and LDA (Learning Disabilities Association) among others.

ATTORNEY'S ROLE

1. Insure that those unable to understand or insist on services receive those privileges guaranteed under our Constitution and federal statutes.

2. Serve as the instrument through which changes are made which will ultimately better serve our children and thus our country.

3. Insure that new thoughts, new goals and new ideas receive appropriate governmental response and funding.

MEDIA'S ROLE

1. Investigate ADHD as it affects American children and American education.

2. Raise public awareness and consciousness.

3. Present both sides of any controversial issues.

PSYCHOLOGICAL/PSYCHOEDUCATIONAL EVALUATION

If a psychologist is contacted by a student's parents to be part of the Team, she will more than likely conduct a complete Psychological/ Psychoeducational Evaluation. The information gathered can help all members of the Team to understand the full implications of ADHD on the intellectual, academic, social, emotional and family life of the ADHD student. Parents are encouraged to share results of the evaluation with their child's teacher.

The following report on John is given to familiarize you with the content and form of this important process.

"Never have ideas about children - and never have ideas for them." D. H. Lawrence, FANTASIA OF THE UNCONSCIOUS 1922

A CASE HISTORY:

THE STORY OF JOHN

John, a seventh grader, age 13 years, 7 months, was referred by his parents, at the suggestion of his teacher, for an in-depth Psychological/ Psychoeducational Evaluation. Problems reported included:

1) Poor grades. John was making C's, D's and F's in content courses, but doing well in others.

2) Interaction problems with teachers. John's mother's comment is noteworthy: "John mirrors the personality of the teacher. His sixth grade science teacher was great. He was great with her. Negative teachers were bad news."

3) Behavioral problems which included:

- Cursing and hitting a child who threw a tennis ball at him - John's mother described the incident as "something snapped." Two days at the detention center was the punishment.

- Stink bomb - Three days suspension at home.

- Impulsively threw a classmate's shoe out the bus window and hit a car breaking a window. Barely avoided a lawsuit.

While John was truly sorry for each incident, there were no real changes in his behavior.

John's parents were distraught and the last episode was the final straw. They felt they had to obtain effective intervention from an ADHD specialist. The more familiar they had become with this constellation of difficulties, the more certain they were that intensive and special ADHD assistance was needed.

Teacher and parent data are presented on subsequent pages to illustrate behavioral profiles and parent and teacher comments typical for many children and adolescents with ADHD. They also demonstrate the helpfulness of the behavioral and academic information you provide in the evaluation process.

Student's Name _____ Homeroom _____ Teacher _____

Date 4-5-89

Dear Parents:
This is a mid-six weeks report of your child's progress in following subjects:

Subjects	Grade Average	Teacher
English	C	
Math	F	
Science	C	
Social Science	A+	H.E.
Link	A	H.E.

Contributing factors in this average are:

	English	Math	Science	Social Science	Reading	Link	H.E.
1. Does not return signed papers							
2. Does not work to potential			✓				✓
3. Does not follow directions				✓			✓
4. Inattentive	✓	✓					✓
5. Does not complete classwork							
6. Does not complete homework		✓	✓				
7. Does not do classwork carefully		✓	✓	✓			
8. Does not do homework carefully	✓	✓	✓				
9. Does not bring necessary materials to class		✓	✓	✓			✓
10. Misbehavior in class	✓	✓		✓			
11. Needs to study for tests	✓	✓	✓	✓			
12. Does not make up work missed when absent							
13. Excessively absent							

Please work with us in correcting these problems.

SEE REVERSE SIDE FOR COMMENTS AND SIGNATURE

April 27, 1989

Mr.

Per our conversation on 4-21-89

reference grades and
teacher comments.

First six week   74 C-
Second   "   70 D-
Third   "   71 D
Fourth   "   79 C+
Fifth   "   57 F

Comments

_____ does not possess good
study habits, organizational skills
and is not attentive in class. He
wastes time, plays, and talks too
much in class. Lacks in
appreciation for learning Mathematics.
He does not complete class and
homework assignments.

Throughout this school year, he
demonstrated a parasitic dependency
towards his peers to accomplish
classroom tasks.

7/26/89

Mr.

This note is in response to your request for comment on classroom behavior. ___ is a capable student and has the ability, I feel, to do much better than he chose to date. ___ is inattentive; he talks, draws, and plays constantly while he should be doing his work. Whenever his name is placed on the board for breaking one of the posted classroom rules, I will deny any wrong doing.

One example of ___ ability to do his social studies work was this oral report. ___ was prepared, including visual aids, and gave a very good report on the state of Virginia. But as a general rule, he does not study for test and do his homework on time.

___ tends to work very hard to improve his classroom behavior and his general deportment. When distractions start to interrupt or influence the class, I have no other choice except to

order that all concerned may complete the assigned work.

Again, ___ has the ability to do better classwork. However, he must improve his behavior, study for test and complete his homework on time. I hope that may in time. Comments have been helpful and can help. If I can be of further assistance, please let me know.

FIRST STATE

5th Semester Grades

English   C/78
80,91,79,83,90,57,64,100,86

Social Studies D/70
64,75,80,91,65,40,72

SPI

COPELAND SYMPTOM CHECKLIST FOR ATTENTION DEFICIT DISORDERS

Attention Deficit Hyperactivity Disorder (ADHD)
and
Undifferentiated Attention Deficit Disorder (ADD)

This checklist was developed from the experience of many specialists in the field of Attention Deficit Disorders and Hyperactivity. It is designed to help you assess whether your child/student has ADHD or ADD, to what degree, and if so, in which area(s) difficulties are experienced. Please mark all statements. Thank you for your assistance in completing this information.

Name of Child _____

Completed by _____ Date _____

Directions: Place a checkmark (✓) by each item below, indicating the degree to which the behavior is characteristic of your child/student.

• denotes ADD with Hyperactivity (ADHD)
•• denotes ADD without Hyperactivity (Undifferentiated ADD)

I. INATTENTION/DISTRACTIBILITY

	Not at all	Just a little	Pretty much	Very much
•• 1. A short attention span, especially for low-interest activities.				✓
•• 2. Difficulty completing tasks.				✓
• 3. Daydreaming.			✓	
• 4. Easily distracted.		✓		
•• 5. Nicknames such as: "spacey," or "dreamer".		✓		
•• 6. Engages in much activity but accomplishes little.			✓	
• 7. Enthusiastic beginnings but poor endings.				✓

Score 16 / 21 — 74 %

II. IMPULSIVITY

	Not at all	Just a little	Pretty much	Very much
• 1. Excitability.			✓	
• 2. Low frustration tolerance.				✓
• 3. Acts before thinking.			✓	
• 4. Disorganization.				✓
• 5. Poor planning ability.			✓	
• 6. Excessively shifts from one activity to another.			✓	
• 7. Difficulty in group situations which require patience and taking turns.				✓
• 8. Requires much supervision.				✓
• 9. Constantly in trouble for deeds of omission as well as deeds of commission.				✓
• 10. Frequently interrupts conversations; talks out of turn.				✓

Score 27 / 30 — 90 %

III. ACTIVITY LEVEL PROBLEMS

A. Overactivity/Hyperactivity

	Not at all	Just a little	Pretty much	Very much
• 1. Restlessness — either fidgetiness or being constantly on the go.				✓
• 2. Diminished need for sleep.		✓		
• 3. Excessive talking.			✓	
• 4. Excessive running, jumping and climbing.			✓	
• 5. Motor restlessness during sleep. Kicks covers off — moves around constantly.				✓
• 6. Difficulty staying seated at meals, in class, etc. Often walks around classroom.			✓	

Score 14 / 18 — 77 %

B. Underactivity

	Not at all	Just a little	Pretty much	Very much
• 1. Lethargy.		✓		
• 2. Daydreaming, spaciness.			✓	
• 3. Failure to complete tasks.			✓	
• 4. Inattention.				✓
• 5. Poor leadership ability.		✓		
• 6. Difficulty in learning and performing.				✓

Score 12 / 18 — 67 %

IV. NON-COMPLIANCE

	Not at all	Just a little	Pretty much	Very much
•• 1. Frequently disobeys.			✓	
• 2. Argumentative.				✓
• 3. Disregards socially-accepted standards of behavior.				✓
•• 4. "Forgets" unintentionally.				✓
• 5. Uses "forgetting" as an excuse (intentional).				✓

Score 12 / 15 — 80 %

Copyright ©1987 by Edna D. Copeland, Ph.D.
Published by SPI Southeastern Psychological Institute, P.O. Box 12389, Atlanta, Georgia 30355-2389

COPELAND SYMPTOM CHECKLIST FOR ATTENTION DEFICIT DISORDERS (Continued)

V. ATTENTION-GETTING BEHAVIOR

	Not at all	Just a little	Pretty much	Very much
• 1. Frequently needs to be the center of attention.				✓
• 2. Constantly asks questions or interrupts.			✓	
• 3. Irritates and annoys siblings, peers and adults.		✓		
• 4. Behaves as the "class clown."		✓		
• 5. Uses bad or rude language to attract attention.		✓		
• 6. Engages in other negative behaviors to attract attention.		✓		

Score 11 / 18 — 61 %

VI. IMMATURITY

	Not at all	Just a little	Pretty much	Very much
• 1. Behavior resembles that of a younger child. Responses are typical of children 6 months to 2-plus years younger.				✓
• 2. Physical development is delayed.		✓		
• 3. Prefers younger children and relates better to them.		✓		
• 4. Emotional reactions are often immature.			✓	

Score 8 / 12 — 67 %

VII. POOR ACHIEVEMENT/COGNITIVE & VISUAL-MOTOR PROBLEMS

	Not at all	Just a little	Pretty much	Very much
•• 1. Underachieves relative to ability.				✓
•• 2. Loses books, assignments, etc.				✓
•• 3. Auditory memory and auditory processing problems.			✓	
•• 4. Learning disabilities/learning problems.			✓	
•• 5. Incomplete assignments.				✓
•• 6. Academic work completed too slowly.			✓	
•• 7. Academic work completed too quickly.		✓		
•• 8. "Messy" or "sloppy" written work; poor handwriting.				✓
•• 9. Poor memory for directions, instructions and rote learning.				✓

Score 22 / 27 — 81 %

VIII. EMOTIONAL DIFFICULTIES

	Not at all	Just a little	Pretty much	Very much
•• 1. Frequent and unpredictable mood swings.			✓	
•• 2. High levels of irritability.			✓	
•• 3. Underactive to pain/insensitive to danger.		✓		
•• 4. Easily overstimulated. Hard to calm down once over-excited.			✓	
•• 5. Low frustration tolerance.			✓	
•• 6. Temper tantrums, angry outbursts.		✓		
•• 7. Moodiness.		✓		
•• 8. Low self-esteem.				✓

Score 15 / 24 — 63 %

IX. POOR PEER RELATIONS

	Not at all	Just a little	Pretty much	Very much
• 1. Hits, bites, or kicks other children.				✓
• 2. Difficulty following the rules of games and social interactions.			✓	
• 3. Rejected or avoided by peers.				✓
• 4. Avoids group activities; a loner.			✓	
• 5. Teases peers and siblings excessively.				✓
• 6. Bullies or bosses other children.				✓

Score 7 / 18 — 39 %

X. FAMILY INTERACTION PROBLEMS

Reported by Mother

	Not at all	Just a little	Pretty much	Very much
• 1. Frequent family conflict.				✓
• 2. Activities and social gatherings are unpleasant.				✓
• 3. Parents argue over discipline since nothing works.				✓
• 4. Mother spends hours and hours on homework with ADD child leaving little time for others in family.			✓	
• 5. Meals are frequently unpleasant.				✓
• 6. Arguments occur between parents and child over responsibilities and chores.				✓
• 7. Stress is continuous from child's social and academic problems.				✓

8. Parents, especially mother, feel:

☒ frustrated ☐ hopeless ☐ alone
☒ angry ☒ guilty ☒ afraid for child
☒ helpless ☒ disappointed ☒ sad and depressed

Score 23 / 24 — 96 %

Copyright ©1987 by Edna D. Copeland, Ph.D.
Published by SPI Southeastern Psychological Institute, P.O. Box 12389, Atlanta, Georgia 30355-2389

62

Teacher's Questionnaire

Name of Child: __John__   Grade __7__

Date of Evaluation: __3-28-89__

Please answer all questions. Beside *each* item, indicate the degree of the problem by a check mark (✓).

	Not at all	Just a little	Pretty much	Very much
1. Restless in the "squirmy" sense.				✓
2. Makes inappropriate noises when he shouldn't.			✓	
3. Demands must be met immediately.				✓
4. Acts "smart" (impudent or sassy).				✓
5. Temper outbursts and unpredictable behavior.			✓	
6. Overly sensitive to criticism.				✓
7. Distractibility or attention span a problem.				✓
8. Disturbs other children.				✓
9. Daydreams.			✓	
10. Pouts and sulks.				✓
11. Mood changes quickly and drastically.				✓
12. Quarrelsome.			✓	
13. Submissive attitude toward authority.	✓			
14. Restless, always "up and on the go."				✓
15. Excitable, impulsive.				✓
16. Excessive demands for teacher's attention.			✓	
17. Appears to be unaccepted by group.		✓		
18. Appears to be easily led by other children.			✓	
19. No sense of fair play.			✓	
20. Appears to lack leadership.				✓
21. Fails to finish things that he starts.				✓
22. Childish and immature.				✓
23. Denies mistakes or blames others.				✓
24. Does not get along well with other children.	✓			
25. Uncooperative with classmates.		✓		
26. Easily frustrated in efforts.			✓	
27. Uncooperative with teacher.				✓
28. Difficulty in learning.				✓

Parent's Questionnaire

Name of Child: _____ John _____   Date: _____

Please answer all questions. Beside *each* item below, indicate the degree of the problem by a check mark (✓).

	Not at all	Just a little	Pretty much	Very much
1. Picks at things (nails, fingers, hair, clothing).		✔		
2. Sassy to grown-ups.		✔		
3. Problems with making or keeping friends.	✔			
4. Excitable, impulsive.				✔
5. Wants to run things.	✔			
6. Sucks or chews (thumb; clothing; blankets).	✔			
7. Cries easily or often.	✔			
8. Carries a chip on his shoulder.	✔			
9. Daydreams.			✔	
10. Difficulty in learning.			✔	
11. Restless in the "squirmy" sense.		✔		
12. Fearful (of new situations; new people or places; going to school).	✔			
13. Restless, always up and on the go.			✔	
14. Destructive.	✔			
15. Tells lies or stories that aren't true.		✔		
16. Shy.	✔			
17. Gets into more trouble than others same age.			✔	
18. Speaks differently from others same age (baby talk; stuttering; hard to understand).	✔			
19. Denies mistakes or blames others.				✔
20. Quarrelsome.			✔	
21. Pouts and sulks.	✔			
22. Steals.	✔			
23. Disobedient or obeys but resentfully.			✔	
24. Worries more than others (about being alone; illness or death).	✔			
25. Fails to finish things.				✔
26. Feelings easily hurt.	✔			
27. Bullies others.	✔			
28. Unable to stop a repetitive activity.	✔			
29. Cruel.	✔			
30. Childish or immature (wants help he shouldn't need; clings; needs constant reassurance).	✔			
31. Distractibility or attention span a problem.				✔
32. Headaches.		✔		
33. Mood changes quickly and drastically.		✔		
34. Doesn't like or doesn't follow rules or restrictions.				✔
35. Fights constantly.	✔			
36. Doesn't get along well with brothers or sisters.		✔		
37. Easily frustrated in efforts.			✔	
38. Disturbs other children.			✔	
39. Basically an unhappy child.		✔		
40. Problems with eating (poor appetite; up between bites).	✔			
41. Stomachaches.	✔			
42. Problems with sleep (can't fall asleep; up too early; up in the night).		✔		
43. Other aches and pains.	✔			
44. Vomiting or nausea.	✔			
45. Feels cheated in family circle.			✔	
46. Boasts and brags.	✔			
47. Lets self be pushed around.	✔			
48. Bowel problems (frequently loose; irregular habits; constipation).	✔			

The questionnaires and teachers' comments reflected John's difficulties: borderline to failing grades; major problems in inattention/distractibility; impulsivity; restlessness with both underactivity and overactivity; noncompliance; and interaction problems with teachers. John's relationships with peers were, for the most part, good and few problems were noted in attention-getting behavior, immaturity, and emotional difficulties. John's social/ emotional development, which had been progressing well, was beginning to reveal signs of stress.

John was evaluated over several hours. The following data sources were utilized:

> Clinical Interview with parents
> Clinical Observations of John
> Wechsler Intelligence Scale for Children-Revised (WISC-R)
> Beery-Buktenica Developmental Test of Visual-Motor Integration
> Detroit Tests of Learning Aptitude
> Wide Range Achievement Test
> Burks' Behavior Rating Scales
> Connor's Parent and Teacher Questionnaires
> Sentence Completion test
> Children's Manifest Anxiety Scale-Revised
> Informal Testing
> Tests of Written Language
> Key Math Test
> Survey of Study Habits and Attitudes
> Learning Style Inventory

John's developmental/educational history was classically ADHD and is as follows:

John is the younger of two children in the family. His brother is 16 years of age. John is the product of a relatively normal pregnancy and delivery. There were no post-delivery complications. As an infant, John was restless, reacted poorly to change in routine, and was very intense. He was unpredictable in feeding and sleeping and was sensitive to noise and light. Due to chronic ear infections, John was overall an unhappy baby. Develop-mental milestones were reached at an early to normal age. His coordination was described as good to average in all areas with the exception of writing, which was noted to be poor. He enjoys basketball and baseball.

Medical history includes chronic ear infections from a very early age. Tubes were placed in his ears at three years of age. John also had allergic reactions to a variety of substances, including many foods. He took allergy shots from the ages of 8 months to 4 years.

John has had some difficulty in school since the first grade. Staying on task, completing assignments, impulsivity, and conflict with teachers have been ongoing problems for John. His work has usually been described as "messy;" he has had difficulty comprehending academic material; and he has had trouble participating in groups. He has had difficulty following directions and organizing tasks and materials. John is currently in the 7th grade. His teachers noted that he is distractible, has a short attention span, has difficulty with academic subjects, especially math and reading, and has difficulty waiting his turn. John currently enjoys going to school, for he likes the social interaction. He does not enjoy the academic work and does not show much interest in it. He has been tutored in math and reading for three summers. He qualifies for the Learning Disabilities Program in math at school. He has been in the program since the 4th grade.

John seeks relationships with peers and is sought by others for friendships. At home the parents noted that John has a high activity level, poor attention span, is impulsive, and has a low frustration threshold. He often exhibits outbursts of temper, interrupts frequently, doesn't listen when spoken to, and has poor memory skills. John appears heedless to danger, and is more active than his brother. He enjoys playing basketball and other outdoor activities. He is a very charming, social young man who loves interaction with others. John dislikes being confined on rainy days. He also dislikes school work and chores.

Test Interpretation

Only portions of the test data will be discussed, those that represent a classic pattern of ADHD. They are as follows:

INTELLECTUAL EVALUATION (WISC-R)

VERBAL TESTS	Scaled Score	Percentile	Range
Information	12	75	High Average
Similarities	13	84	High Average
*Arithmetic	7	16	Low Average
Vocabulary	11	63	Average
Comprehension	14	91	Superior
*Digit Span	9	37	Average

PERFORMANCE TESTS	Scaled Score	Percentile	Range
Picture Completion	15	95	Very Superior
Picture Arrangement	13	84	High Average
Block Design	9	37	Average
Object Assembly	13	84	High Average
*Coding	7	16	Low Average
Mazes	13	84	High Average

Verbal I.Q. Score	=	109 - 72nd Percentile, High Average Range
Performance I.Q. Score	=	109 - 72nd Percentile, Average Range
Full Scale I.Q. Score	=	109 - 72nd Percentile, High Average Range
Distractibility Quotient(*)	=	85 - 16th Percentile, Low Average Range
Potential I.Q. (Based on Scores not Affected by the ADHD)	=	115 - 119, 84th to 90th Percentile

Summary of Intellectual Assessment: Results of the intellectual evaluation indicate that John is currently functioning overall at the high end of the Average range of mental abilities. There was not a significant discrepancy between his language abilities and visual/spatial abilities. There was, however, significant variability among the subtest scores. The pattern of scores reflects interference, as well as potential higher than the scores obtained. A distractibility quotient was computed. This is an IQ equivalency score which frequently predicts the child's level of academic achievement better than IQ scores. This score was 85, and indicates that John's short attention span, distractibility and impulsivity interfered with his performance on this test. Therefore, the I.Q. scores obtained should be considered underestimates of his true ability. Areas of comparative strength identified were his common-sense reasoning and judgment, alertness to visual detail, abstract verbal reasoning, and long-term visual memory. Areas of comparative weakness noted were his short-term auditory memory, mental computation, and concentration. John's speed and accuracy in executing visual-motor tasks is significantly delayed and suggests grapho-motor problems and an excessively slow work rate. The scores obtained in this evaluation are consistent with those obtained in the fourth grade. John has a significant problem with internal distractibility. His distractibility quotient is noteworthy in that it is 24 points below his Full Scale I.Q. score and 30 points below his true potential.

By third or fourth grade a student's level of distractibility usually determines academic performance more than does intellectual ability. This was certainly true for John:

WIDE RANGE ACHIEVEMENT TEST (WRAT-R)

	Standard Score	Percentile	Grade Equivalent
Reading	80	9	4-E
Spelling	86	18	5-E
Arithmetic	75	5	5-E

John's achievement is consistent with his Distractibility Quotient, not his intellectual ability. There is, in fact, a discrepancy of 23 to 34 points between ability and achievement in all three measures reported. While John qualifies for LD, it is the Examiner's opinion that the problem is more ADHD than LD.

Auditory and Visual Memory

Measures of short-term visual and auditory memory are also negatively affected by the ADHD and are often hallmarks in the diagnosis. John's scores were again typical and are as follows:

	Age Equivalent	Difference From Chrono-logic Age
WISC-R SS = 9, 37th Percentile		
Digit Span (Memory for Numbers)		
Detroit Test of Learning Aptitudes		
Auditory Attention Span for Unrelated Words (Memory for Nonmeaningful Material)	7.9	-5.10 yrs
Auditory Attention Span for Related Syllables (Memory for Meaningful Material)	11.6	-2.1 yrs
Visual Attention Span for Letters	9.6-9.9	-4.0 yrs.
Oral Directions	6.0	-7.0 yrs-7 mos

All areas of memory were very negatively affected by the attentional deficits. On the Detroit Tests of Learning Aptitude short-term auditory memory scores ranged from 7 years-9 months of age to 11 years-6 months of age. These scores are 5 years-10 months to 2 years-1 month delayed. Short-term visual memory was also negatively affected by the attentional problems. These scores ranged from 9 years-6 months to 9 years-9 months of age. When material was presented auditorially and visually simultaneously, performance was even more impaired. These scores were at 6 years of age, which is 7 years-7 months delayed. Long-term auditory and visual memory were much stronger areas for John. Scores in these areas were in the high average to superior ranges of ability.

Long-term memory is less affected by ADHD than short-term memory, although negative effects are seen in cumulative tests and exams. Even very bright ADHD students often do very poorly, for their ability level, on the Scholastic Achievement Test (SAT), which is a measure of acquired knowledge and retention of information. Thus, the ADHD problems continue to haunt them. Interference in John's ability to retain information, for example, was profound and resulted in drastic underachievement. The distractibility quotient (DQ) correctly predicted his level of academic achievement which was in the 75-86 standard score range. His achievement scores were thus approximately 23-34 standard score points below expectancy.

Attention, Concentration and Impulse Control

Attention, concentration and impulse control are essential to the learning process. When there are difficulties in any of these areas, learning is adversely affected because the child lacks the ability to sustain his attention, to concentrate his efforts, and to discipline himself adequately to perform the exercises necessary to *lock* knowledge into long-term memory. By third grade, and often before, these difficulties have caused the child to underachieve significantly in relation to potential.

Questionnaires were completed by John's parents and teachers to help determine whether difficulties concentrating and controlling his impulses were present, as well as other attention deficit symptoms.

As previously stated, John's teachers perceived him as having major difficulty completing tasks and following directions in the classroom. He was described as impulsive, distractible, and easily frustrated. John was also seen as having difficulty listening attentively to oral discussions and directions and as quite disorganized. John did not work well independently. On the Symptom Checklist for Attention Deficit Disorders major problems areas were seen in inattention/distractibility, impulsivity, overactivity, and attention-getting behaviors. Immaturity, poor peer relations and emotional difficulties were not reported. Poor school achievement, especially in the area of visual-motor skills, was also present. As mentioned previously, it was apparent from clinical observations and talking with John that he had major problems with internal distractibility. These occurred in the tightly controlled one-on-one testing setting and were quite obvious from his self-descriptions of class and home concentration. Impulsivity was also present. Based on teacher and parent reports, clinical observations, and test results, it was the Examiner's opinion that John had a significant Attention Deficit Disorder without Hyperactivity, which had resulted in much frustration, significant underachievement, loss of confidence, and a tendency to remain at a superficial level in most of his interactions.

Social/Emotional Development

Social/emotional development is usually affected by the ADHD difficulties. While John had escaped major problems in this area, the ADHD had taken some toll. The report was as follows:

John is a sweet, sensitive, outgoing child, who is basically emotionally healthy. He is experiencing many of the symptoms of the Attention Deficit Disorder and the academic and emotional difficulties that follow. Distracti-bility, short attention span, and lack of continuity of effort and perseverance are significant problems and are negatively impacting his academic performance, resulting in extremely poor acquisition of academic skills. John is an extraverted adolescent who relates well to peers and is liked by most. He loves people and enjoys social situations. At times, however, John has difficulty relating to figures of authority and is easily led by others in groups. He is beginning to show indications of lack of confidence and anxiety about himself. He has a low frustration threshold and can become upset easily. He acts out on occasion and engages in immature behaviors both impulsively and to gain attention. John has begun to blame himself to some degree but has not withdrawn, nor has he become overly aggressive toward others. He complies with most social expectations, although he engages in impulsive and inappropriate behaviors which could have major social and even legal consequences. John's difficulties have produced some problems at home where his forgetfulness, disorganization, and inability to stay on task have been very frustrating.

Study habits and attitudes toward education and teachers are usually negatively affected by the ADHD. John's scores in all areas, except desire for teacher approval, were below the 10th percentile. His desire for teacher acceptance was at the 25th percentile. John's "Survey of Study Habits and Attitudes" revealed procrastination in completing assignments, inefficient study habits and a general rejection of both teachers, their classroom methods and fundamental educational objectives, practices and requirements.

John's school experiences have not been positive. It is understandable that he has not embraced educational objectives. However, to be successful, it will be necessary to change both his attitudes and his study habits. Students with profiles as low as his generally perform poorly in school.

Results of the High School Personality Questionnaire were basically positive. This self-report questionnaire revealed John to be a warm, outgoing, social person who is cheerful and enthusiastic, although somewhat impulsive; as one who can deal with stress well; and one who is venturesome in his attitude. John rated himself as somewhat undisciplined and one who could become too easily annoyed and emotional. While these traits need attention, the positive aspects of his personality certainly outweigh the negative.

Social/emotional development is usually delayed and/or problematic in most ADHD students. John did not fit this pattern to the degree seen in most students who have experienced ADHD symptoms and school difficulties for this long. Rather, the positive support of his family, his gregarious personality and his athletic skills had enabled him to succeed socially until the 7th grade. John is an excellent example of how supportive people in a student's environment can mitigate some of the effects of the ADHD problems.

Recommendations

On the basis of the evaluation, several recommendations were made:

1. The Attention Deficit Disorder should receive treatment. Current treatment approaches include the use of:(a) stimulant medication (Ritalin, Dexedrine or Cylert) which stimulates the sluggish Reticular Activating System and other attention centers of the brain to organize and integrate stimuli and responses more effectively; (b) behavior management strategies; (c) educational intervention; (d) psychosocial interventions, and (e) for a few children, dietary intervention.

    a) All of the above treatment approaches were discussed. Behavior management strategies are essential both at home and at school. These were reviewed in detail. At home the parents were encouraged to use the Thinking Room and the writing of sentences or essays for inappropriate behavior, and a Responsibility/Behavior Chart to let John know exactly what was expected of him. A point reinforcement system was encouraged so that John could begin not only to accept responsibility and limits, but could enjoy the benefits of self-determination and the ability to achieve his goals by accommodating to the necessary parental and school expectations placed on him. Behavior management strategies for school were also discussed and a program implemented.

        Regardless of other treatments, helping John develop responsibility, internal self-control, and self-discipline, and coming to terms with adult authority will be essential. Likewise, John's difficulty with organizational skills, attention to detail and follow-through will be assisted by the responsibility charts and programs recommended. You must be very firm, expect these things from John and utilize both the positive and negative consequences resulting from his behavior consistently. Adolescents on these programs generally perform well and are pleased with their accomplishments.

    b) Many children with ADHD have allergies. John does appear to have significant allergic involvement. You may wish to consider an Elimination and Challenge Diet to determine any food intolerances that may not have already been diagnosed by his allergist. While it is a somewhat strenuous family commitment for four to six weeks, most parents find it well worth the effort and can, with peace of mind, rule it in or out as a causative factor in their child's attention deficit disorder. The area of food intolerance is somewhat controversial. Our clinical experience, however, as well as the work of others, suggests that it is an approach without expense or danger that can produce significant benefit. If in doubt, discuss its merits with others whose judgment you trust. For some children, it reduces the need for medical intervention. Thus, it is especially recommended for those parents who hope to avoid using medication in the treatment of their child's attention deficit disorder. John's other allergies must constantly be kept under control as well.

c) The educational issues, of course, must be addressed (see Recommendation #2).

d) If all of the above measures do not produce satisfactory results in four to six weeks, you are encouraged to consult your pediatrician and discuss the use of medication with him. Stimulant and other medications are utilized with ADHD children, adolescents and adults with great success. You are also encouraged to learn as much as possible about the treatment of ADHD and the medication controversy so as to be informed of all the parameters involved in its use. Only informed parents can make wise decisions about treating their ADHD child.

2. John needs immediate and intense learning disabilities assistance. While his academic delays may well be a function of the ADHD, at this time they are so great that he qualifies for learning disability assistance in all areas. With much individualized instruction in conjunction with treatment of the ADHD, great progress should occur. He may require LD assistance throughout this summer and next year.

3. A summer camp was suggested to you which offers an outstanding program of individualized study in content areas as well as much assistance with study skills, organization and responsibility.

4. John's short-term visual memory is delayed and should be addressed, for it will cause significant problems in the acquisition and retention of academic skills requiring visually acquired information. John's delayed reading is believed partially a function of this factor. While treatment of the ADHD should benefit short-term visual memory, you are encouraged to do the following:

a) Utilize additional visual repetition. Put the information to be learned on 3x5 cards and expose John to limited amounts of information repeatedly - in the car, on the refrigerator, before bed, etc. For example, put three spelling words, algebra equations, or history facts on cards and repeat those until they are "locked in" to his visual memory bank. Then take three more. Daily review of all is helpful for greatest retention.

b) Computer instruction is also quite beneficial for the child with visual learning requirements.

c) Language strategies to help the child remember are especially helpful for strong auditory learners like John.

5.   John will probably always think faster than he can write and thus may find writing frustrating and cumbersome as the volume increases. For that reason, you are encouraged to teach him typing and word processing as soon as possible. Most children can learn to type as early as kindergarten. Many programs offer typing for 4th grade students and older. Word processing is also extremely helpful later on. Typing and word processing free up the creativity and initiative of many children, especially those with ADHD and poor fine-motor development. A multi-sensory approach to handwriting is also recommended. This approach is especially beneficial to ADHD students who benefit from the involvement of all senses in the learning process.

John has been in treatment for approximately ten months. He was placed on medication, initially Ritalin. However, it was not effective: "It makes me sick at my stomach and I feel 'funny'." Therefore, he was switched to Dexedrine Spansule, to which he has responded quite well.

In addition to the medication, John has been on an intensive Responsibility Program. A Behavior Management Program for his difficulties was also instituted. Additional tutorial assistance was obtained and John will no longer require LD services after this year. Family therapy, as needed, has been utilized. The other recommendations have also been implemented.

John's principal was so pleased with his progress that she wrote him a letter of commendation after three months of treatment.

At this time John and his parents continue to struggle to some degree with the ADHD. However, he has not had a detention this year and has no grade lower than a "C". Most are B's, in fact. The issues which do arise are typical adolescent struggles, compounded slightly by the ADHD. Both John and his parents enjoy life more now and feel very optimistic about his future.

"I always tell students that it is what you learn after you know it all that counts." Harry S. Truman

TREATMENT APPROACHES FOR ATTENTION DISORDERS

Attention disorders have been subjected to rigorous and intensive investigation for the last two decades. They have been especially prominent disorders, both clinically and experimentally, since 1980 when officially labeled "ADD" by the American Psychiatric Association.

The most important information to surface from the vast array of research and clinical experience over the last twenty years is that no treatment approach for ADHD is successful alone. Medicine alone produces no more benefit by adolescence than not treating the child at all. On the other hand, psychological and educational interventions are often not effective without medication. It appears that medicine enables many children and adolescents to benefit from interventions which would not be effective without it.

With this in mind, we encourage treating the *whole* child. Only a multimodal approach will insure improvement, not only in your classroom, but for the rest of your student's life. It is important to encourage each family to study the various treatment approaches available to them and to choose the ones with which they are the most comfortable. Parents have often been negatively influenced and refused treatments based on their lack of knowledge or misunderstanding. Educating the parents of ADHD children is essential.

STIMULANT AND OTHER MEDICATIONS

For the last fifty years, professionals and parents have been treating children with ADHD with a variety of approaches. While most have offered some assistance, the one which appears to have consistently been the most helpful is the use of stimulant medication. Research shows that for a great percentage of those diagnosed with physiological ADHD, medication is an appropriate and effective treatment choice. However, of all the treatment approaches available for ADHD, choosing to use medication is often the most difficult decision for parents to make. When given adequate information, however, many parents decide that treating the whole child--medically, socially, psychologically and emotionally--will ultimately result in promoting the self-esteem, competence, organization and cooperative spirit necessary to insure their child's success for a lifetime.

GOAL OF MEDICATION

The goal of all medications used to treat ADHD is to help the brain function efficiently and effectively. Just as glasses correct vision, medication corrects the neurochemical imbalances causing the ADHD symptoms. Medication used with ADHD children does not have a *drugging effect* like a tranquilizer. Rather, it regulates the child's brain chemistry so that he can function properly.

Neither does medicine change the child's basic personality or values. Children and adolescents treated with medication are simply better able to accomplish what they want to do. The treatment does not force a child to be good. It does enable him to exercise the self-control, attention to task, persistence and thoughtfulness necessary to function normally in academic and social situations. In our experience, every ADHD student wants to be in control and to be successful.

HOW DOES MEDICINE WORK?

While the exact mechanisms are not completely understood, it is widely accepted in scientific circles that physiological ADHD is a result of deficiencies and/or imbalances in neurotransmitters, or brain chemicals.

Current evidence indicates that stimulant medication alters neurochemical imbalances and blood flow to particular regions, resulting in improved functioning in the frontal and central brain structures important in alertness and attention. As medication improves brain functioning, there is a corresponding improvement in the student's ability to attend and in his impulse control, behavior, cooperativeness, reasonableness, and sensitivity to social cues and expectations. A positive change in alertness is noted in the underactive, daydreaming ADHD child or adolescent, while increased attention and decreased activity and restlessness are noted in the overactive ADHD student. Academic improvement is almost always noted, as well as improved behavior, peer relations, student-teacher relations, and family interactions. Sports, music and other nonacademic activities are also positively affected.

CHOOSING THE RIGHT MEDICATION

Even though professionals who have worked with ADHD children for a long time often have an intuitive sense of what will be effective, deciding on a particular medication is largely a trial-and-error procedure. The most commonly used medications are methylphenidate (Ritalin) and dextroamphetamine (Dexedrine), with Ritalin being prescribed more frequently than Dexedrine. Dexedrine has been used since 1937, while Ritalin was approved for use with children in 1961.

Cylert is another stimulant medication that is the most recently available. A much less commonly used stimulant medication is methamphetamine (Desoxyn). Little information exists on the long-term effects of Cylert and Desoxyn. By contrast, both Ritalin and Dexedrine have been used for many years with studies showing no apparent major long-term problems with use.

The physician monitoring your student's treatment will start the medicine in low doses and increase it gradually. If the student does not respond to one medicine, he may well respond to another. It may take several weeks to establish the optimum medication, dosage and time intervals taken.

STIMULANT MEDICATIONS

FIRST-LINE MEDICATIONS

Ritalin (Methylphenidate hydrochloride) is the most commonly used stimulant medication and the one frequently tried first. A great percentage of those with whom it is tried find it effective.

Ritalin is available in a *short-acting* tablet form which lasts approximately three to five hours, depending upon individual metabolism. It is also available in a *long-acting*, time-release 20 mg. tablet (SR-20) that lasts approximately seven to ten hours depending upon individual metabolism. It is the approximate equivalent of a 10 mg. tablet taken twice daily. However, the SR-20 may not produce the same benefit as two 10 mg. tablets given at breakfast and noon. It should be monitored very carefully since it may metabolize unevenly in some children.

Dexedrine (Dextroamphetamine sulfate) is not used as commonly as Ritalin but some children, adolescents and adults respond better to it than to Ritalin. It is available in 5 mg. short-acting tablets. Long-acting spansules, in 5, 10 and 15 mg., are also available. They are time-release and last approximately seven to twelve hours.

Cylert (Pemoline) is a relatively new medication and researchers know the least about its potential long-term effects and benefits. It is available in 18.5, 37.5, and 75 mg. tablets. It is generally tried after Ritalin and Dexedrine have been found unsuccessful. For a few children, however, it appears to be a very effective medication.

SIDE EFFECTS OF RITALIN AND DEXEDRINE

Almost every medicine does have side effects. Whenever there is a medical problem, each person must make a choice between living with the medical disorder or the potential side effects of treatment. Many parents have decided that the side effects of medicine are far less negative than the disorder. It is the improper use of stimulants, whether through misdiagnosis or overdosage, that has caused most of the problems so prominent in the adverse publicity surrounding this issue.

1)   *Appetite Suppression.* This is the most frequent side effect cited for both Ritalin and Dexedrine. However, many parents have found that it can be managed. Giving the child breakfast before he takes the medicine will generally cause the morning meal not to be affected. The noon meal is more often a problem than not. You can help your student by encouraging him to eat something, even if he must make himself. A very moderate amount of food will avoid a headache or the irritability that can occur with hunger.

Some concern has been raised over the possibility of growth suppression due to the loss of appetite. This area has been carefully investigated. If growth is slowed down at all, there appears to be a *growth rebound* effect that occurs after a student stops taking the medicine, especially in the summer.

Despite the fairly limited real danger, most physicians check height and weight three to four times a year and obtain an annual CBC and chemical profile. If problems are noted, the stimulants are discontinued. Other medications are usually tried in their place if still needed.

2)   *Sleep Disturbance.* Stimulant medications sometimes cause or increase difficulty falling asleep. When they do, they must be adjusted to avoid this negative effect. Some children actually fall asleep more easily when on medication.

3)   *Increase in Pulse Rate or Blood Pressure.* Stimulants may cause a mild increase in heart rate. When it does occur, it is often a minor increase and does not warrant discontinuation of medication. However, there have been a few cases in which it necessitated a different therapeutic intervention.

4)   *Headaches and Stomachaches.* These are frequent complaints when a child first begins medication. When the medication is started at low doses, however, these negative effects are usually minimal and subside after a few days. If they continue, a change of medication is usually warranted.

5)   *Lethargy, Depression, Becoming "Glassy-eyed" or a "Zombie."* These symptoms are *not* side effects of the medication. Rather, they indicate that the dosage of medication is too high, the child is on the wrong medication for the ADD, or that the diagnosis is incorrect.

6)   *Development of Tics or Tourette's Syndrome.* A few children will develop tics or involuntary muscle movements such as eye-blinking or grimacing when placed on stimulant medication. When this occurs, medication must be reduced or discontinued. You should be very alert to this possible side effect and notify both the student's parents and physician should this occur.

SECOND-TIER MEDICATIONS

Tricyclic antidepressant may be a misnomer for this group of medications used to treat a number of disorders including depression, bedwetting, migraine headaches and attention deficit disorders. Like the stimulants, tricyclic antidepressants affect the neurotransmitters. They appear to prevent the breakdown of selected brain chemicals, leaving more available to stimulate those parts of the brain which control attention, inhibition, vigilance and alertness.

The two most commonly used are Tofranil (Imipramine Hydrochloride) and Norpramine (Desipramine Hydrochloride). Norpramine is a derivative of Tofranil and produces fewer side effects.

Despite their potential risks, most experts consider tricyclic antidepressants a valuable tool in our medicinal arsenal against ADHD and depression. The risk:benefit ratio, however, must be carefully assessed to determine quite definitively that the benefits clearly outweigh the risks.

MEDICATION FOR SPECIAL SITUATIONS

While the following medications are not used as frequently as those in the first or second groups, there are instances where they are beneficial in the overall treatment program of the child.

1) *Clonidine* has been found useful for overfocused children. Stimulant medication, on the other hand, worsens their symptoms markedly. Behavior management strategies, education, and environmental manipulation are also extremely helpful for the overfocused child.

Clonidine has also been found to be helpful in treating children with tics or Tourette's Syndrome, although the research in this area is somewhat inconclusive.

2) *Tegretol*, an anticonvulsant, is used for ADHD children with seizure disorders, especially complex partial seizures, which are manifested primarily in outbursts of aggressive behavior. Children with other seizure disorders may require a combination of anticonvulsants and stimulants.

3) *Major tranquilizers* (neuroleptics), such as the phenothiazines (Mellaril, Thorazine) and haloperidol (Haldol) are used primarily to treat severe psychiatric disorders or students with anxiety so severe that it looks like ADHD. They are generally much less effective than stimulants. Small doses of Haldol, however, are often utilized successfully to treat Tourette's Syndrome.

THE TEACHER'S ROLE

The importance of the teacher's role in monitoring medication cannot be overstated. You are the person who sees the child or adolescent the most when he is on the medication. This is especially true for those students who only take the medicine twice a day, five days a week. Increasingly, however, parents are being encouraged to think of ADHD as a *life* problem and not necessarily just a *school* problem, and medication is given three times a day, seven days a week.

Once a child has been placed on medication, many physicians will send you behavior checklists to mark on a daily basis. A daily checksheet along with your comments helps the physician know exactly how the medicine is affecting your student. These checklists communicate a wealth of essential information and a side-effects checklist (see Appendix) records adverse effects you notice. They also save time and energy trying to make and return phone calls between busy and not easily available professionals (both you and the physician).

If the physician does not contact you, you are encouraged to contact him and advise him of your willingness to be of assistance (see letter in Appendix). Ideally everyone working with the child will have met or teleconferenced at least once before a treatment program is begun. Continue completing the checklists until your student has reached an optimum level of benefit.

BEHAVIOR MANAGEMENT STRATEGIES

Behavior management techniques have been effectively used in child-rearing and teaching for the past twenty years. The goal of most parents and teachers is to teach children and adolescents the behaviors, values, goals, and interpersonal skills which seem worthy to them and to discourage those which they do not value. By reinforcing those things desired through positive reinforcement and incentive, and discouraging those things not wanted through lack of attention, negative reinforcement and even punishment, adults are able to mold and influence children's outcomes.

Most teachers intuitively follow behavioral principles when they are successful. Teachers who are not successful often are using behavioral principles as well. However, they often are inadvertently reinforcing the wrong things, i.e., behaviors and attributes they do *not* want in their students.

Effective behavior management approaches in the classroom have as their goal to assist teachers in selectively reinforcing students' impulse control, self-discipline, organizational skills and conformity to parental, school, and societal expectations through the use of both positive reinforcement for approved behavior and negative consequences for inappropriate behavior. Specific ADHD behaviors can also be addressed, such things as training a student to attend to relevant stimuli; helping him develop a system of *stop, look and listen* to improve his alertness and increase his attention to adults when they speak; to count to three before acting; and to repeat instructions before attempting a task.

Behavior management strategies have a definite and important place in the classroom with ADHD students. Used alone, that is, without medication, they have not been found as effective as medication alone. They can, in fact, be discouraging because of the slow progress the student sometimes makes. Medication and behavior management together, however, have been found to be a winning combination.

Behavior management methods include:

- Positive incentive programs for developing desired behaviors, attitudes and responsibilities.

- Negative reinforcement programs for inappropriate behaviors.

- Organization, responsibility, structure, routine and efficient planning ahead.

ORGANIZATION, STRUCTURE AND ROUTINE

A significant problem area for ADHD students and one addressed by behavior management strategies is that of establishing structure, routines and organizational skills. The Reticular Activating System and prefrontal cortex are responsible for organization, planning, judgment and generally *keeping one's act together*. Since these skills are deficient in the ADHD student, he is notably disorganized, forgetful, and unable to plan ahead and decide upon priorities. Establishing and teaching structure, routine and organization are imperative, for only in this way does the ADHD child internalize the structure he will need for future success.

Structure, however, should not be confused with strictness which implies an inflexibility that does not recognize individual differences and specific situations. ADHD children are often unresponsive to strict rule structures and rebel against them. This is a very natural reaction since they do, in fact, display many individual differences which need to be recognized.

Organize yourself and the class to have a more successful classroom. No student is ever more organized than the teacher! If you want a smoothly running classroom, you must spend time organizing yourself. Some helpful hints include:

1) *Prepare a lesson plan and make sure materials are ready.* Post your own personal schedule on your desk with specific reminders. Try to have all of this completed fifteen minutes before the first child is to arrive. Plan each day for your students and post the schedule on the bulletin board. Keep it as consistent as possible from day to day and week to week.

2) *Spend the first fifteen minutes of each day organizing the children.* First, have each child *clean* his desk or cubby, throwing away trash, putting loose papers in the correct folder, sharpening pencils, etc. Then review the schedule. Highlight any changes or special activities. Have the children recite in unison or separately the routine. Have an organized child, preferably a friend, assist the ADHD child if this task is overwhelming. Utilize a monthly calendar and go over it with your students, discussing special events and the plans which need to be made for them.

3) *Color code the student's books and materials.* It is often helpful to the students to have the books and materials for each subject, including spiral notebooks, all the same color. For example, science books are all red, math is blue, etc.

4) *Post the day's work on the board.* While you are encouraged to post all of the work, you are encouraged not to have them sit and work without interruption for one or more hours. The ADHD student may need a schedule and the assignments posted on his desk as well (see Appendix: "Today's Schedule"). He will work best if the assignments are numbered in priority and he is given a time frame in which to work (see "Assignments for_____ Date_____). Set up a signal

whereby he can notify you as he finishes each task. ADHD children need both frequent breaks and more reinforcement than their non-ADHD peers. After completing two or three assignments, he may signal to you or the assistant to come and check his work.

5) *Have the ADHD student (and all students) have an organized notebook.* A three-ring binder with three pocket folders is ideal for both elementary, middle and high school students. This notebook must go everywhere with the child--to each class and home every day. Make this an absolute essential with positive incentives for remembering and negative ones for not remembering. The three pocket folders are:

> **Work To Be Done** (Includes all homework, incomplete classwork, papers to be signed, etc.)

> **Completed Work** (Includes all completed work and signed papers to be returned to school.)

> **Papers To Save** (Includes completed work that has been corrected to file in a permanent place.)

On the inside of the three-ring notebook have the student scotchtape a new "Homework Assignment Sheet" each week (see Appendix). This sheet is his organizer and will be his salvation. All assignments are recorded ("0" for no assignment); long-term assignments, tests and things to be taken to school or home are written down as well. ADHD students can be very forgetful and disorganized. Have them write things down immediately after directions or assignments have been given. Teaching students organization and planning skills will be of great benefit not only for the student but for you and his parents as well.

When a student is having difficulty, you are encouraged to coordinate your efforts with those of his parents. The children most likely to be successful are those who have parents at home willing to follow through. If a child is having difficulty, the teacher checks the assignments the student has recorded, reminding him of any forgotten ones. She then initials the sheet and adds any comment she feels is appropriate. It is helpful to keep it positive. If a student is having difficulty with the weekly assignment sheet, a daily one can be used (see Appendix). Also, if parents and teachers are commenting daily on progress, a form can be sent home recording daily grades or progress in classwork, homework and tests (see Appendix). Most children improve immediately when this system of organization and parent/teacher checks and balances is instituted. This program is effective for elementary, middle and high school students. Additional subject notebooks are needed for older students, but should not replace THE NOTEBOOK.

6) *Orient the students again after lunch.* Review the schedule, encourage on-task behavior and reward doing one's best. Special treats injected, humorous stories and constant encouragement should punctuate your goal-oriented atmosphere. Also, you may wish to utilize the suggestions in the chapter on classroom management strategies generously throughout the day.

7) *Spend ten minutes organizing again at the end of the day.* Have your students look at their assignment sheets to see what they need to carry home. Many ADHD students in desperation will carry every book home every night so as not to forget something they need. While this approach develops great muscles, it does little to help them better manage their lives.

8) *Organize your ADHD students' families.* You can also help the parents of your students become organized by having a session with them to explain your expectations. Encourage them to monitor their children's notebooks and assignment sheets and to alert you to any concerns. Show them examples of responsibility charts and family calendars (see Appendix) they might like to use at home. Stress the importance of getting the child organized for school at night before he goes to bed. It is also important for them to get the child up early enough to straighten his room,

eat breakfast, plan for the day and get to school early. Arriving at school after quickly throwing down breakfast and rushing all the way is not conducive to a calm, productive school day.

POSITIVE INCENTIVE PROGRAMS FOR

DEVELOPING DESIRED BEHAVIOR

We know that to be truly successful with children we must change <u>attitudes</u> as well as behavior. Positive reinforcement, incentives and encouragement change attitudes <u>and</u> behavior. Punishment temporarily stops negative behavior. It does little at best, however, to effect long-term beneficial changes in attitude. Honey has always been a more effective reinforcer than vinegar!

Establish positive goals for the entire class and incentives for reaching those. Make these group goals which emphasize cooperation and helping everyone to meet the class goals.

When a student is having behavioral difficulty, note the behaviors that are bothering you (see Appendix - "My Student's Behavior"). Analyze the situation carefully and see what triggers the problems. Try to eliminate any causal factors over which you have control. Then meet with the student and discuss the difficulties. Set up an incentive program at school for overcoming the difficulties. You may find the "Daily Progress Reports" in the Appendix helpful.

Most children, even impulsive ADD children, are quite willing to change negative behaviors to achieve what *they* want. Not only does the child earn a positive reward, he also earns your approval and praise. Appropriate behaviors are decided upon and placed on a chart. The behaviors might include getting along with peers, being respectful of you, complying the first time asked, and not interrupting, among others. Examples of typical behaviors of ADHD students are included on the charts in the Appendix.

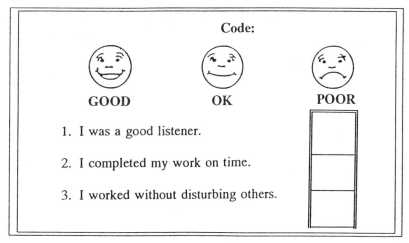

The behavior chart may initially have to be established for short time intervals, such as 15 minutes. The time is gradually extended until it includes an entire morning, afternoon or evening. For appropriate behavior, the child earns chips, checks, smiley faces, or whatever system with which you feel comfortable. Have the student work in the class for a goal he desires: to be the class leader, to peer tutor a classmate or younger child, or to be the messenger for the day. Try utilizing only an incentive program initially. For many children, not receiving a chip, a smiley face or an *Excellent* is punishment enough. Utilize much coaching in appropriate behaviors and as much encouragement as possible. If the only thing you can say about the child is "I like your eyebrows," say it! These are the children who need positives the most.

When negative consequences are necessary, the use of a *Thinking* Chair or *Thinking* Room is encouraged. Writing sentences, an essay about what happened following previously given guidelines, or an action plan, among others, can facilitate the cognitive processing of understanding and subsequently changing inappropriate behavior. It is essential to do this in a positive manner: "Jamie, you're having difficulty with _____. I want you to sit and think (write) about _____ and then we'll talk." Talking about what happened, the student's feelings (or impulses) which led to the behavior, and appropriate ways to handle those feelings (impulses) next time are crucial to this process. Never leave the child without a *true* positive: not "You have so much potential. Why . . . ?" but rather, "I really like you." or "You're such a neat kid; I know we can overcome this together." Remember the meaning of discipline, that is, *to teach*. We *do* want to teach students self-control and appropriate behavior. We do *not* want to teach them to hate school and authorities. How you deal with difficult behavioral issues is a key element in your student's willingness and ability to change and the attitudes he will develop about school.

The essence of behavior management strategies is having desirable and undesirable behaviors well-defined, establishing positive consequences for appropriate behaviors and negative consequences for undesirable behavior, and *consistently* and nonemotionally *enforcing* the consequences. The child is in control of himself. It is *he* who determines the consequences. You are merely the mediator between *his* actions and *his* consequences.

ADHD children require many repetitions of consequences before they learn. However, they do learn if you will not become frustrated and not give up. Most successful teachers of ADHD children often feel more like Army sergeants than the nurturing, adoring adults they dreamed they would be. However, the payoff for you in creating a competent, happy student will be worth a year of *holding the line*.

Most children want, more than anything else, to please their parents and teachers. ADHD children, likewise, do--often even more than others. They develop a sense of internal motivation and satisfaction, however, only after many positive experiences with external limits and rewards. Until that is developed, it is your job as a teacher to motivate your ADHD student through the use of positive and negative consequences for his behavior. The Thinking Room, a positive reinforcement system, writing, incentives and encouragement are far more fulfilling to both you and your student than nagging, criticism, and coercion. The ADHD students you teach will need your ongoing structure, guidance and encouragement to develop the internal controls they lack. They need teachers who will take the time and learn the methods to teach them to behave in ways conducive to their own fulfillment and happiness.

One note of caution: The most positive and encouraging teacher and the very best behavior management program can often not deal effectively with a child with serious physiological problems. It is crucial that you obtain medical assistance for children and adolescents who do not respond to well-designed behavioral intervention programs. You may wish to video some of the student's behavior if parents do not understand. Be certain, first, that your attitudes and methods of dealing with the child are not part of the problem.

"The real menace in dealing with a five-year-old is that in no time at all you begin to sound like a five-year-old." Jean Kerr, PLEASE DON'T EAT THE DAISIES

PSYCHOLOGICAL INTERVENTIONS

While attention deficit disorders are almost universally accepted as physiologically caused, it is clearly apparent that psychological and social variables also play a major role in the student's overall adjustment. Psychological intervention is not only helpful but is necessary for the long-term benefit of the child or adolescent. ADHD students will not only experience the usual disappointments, misbehaviors, altercations and frustrations of school and family life as their peers, but will experience other difficulties unique to their poor attention, impulsivity and impaired activity levels.

COGNITIVE THERAPY IN THE CLASSROOM

The goal of cognitive therapy is to help children and adolescents utilize language for problem-solving rather than to continue their impulsive responding to various situations. It is insufficient alone for the treatment of ADHD. However, it is a very effective intervention when used as part of a multimodal treatment program.

Language is very important in the development of the frontal lobes of the brain, especially inner language. Children and adolescents who talk through a problem mentally before acting do better in school and gain higher-level thinking skills sooner than those who do not. Teachers serve as powerful models of thoughtful behavior. Students often copy the problem-solving strategies they see you employing.

You can assist with the cognitive development of all of the children in your class by helping your students verbalize problems and consciously think through possible solutions. Set up *think-tanks* when problems come up. Have your students individually, then in pairs, small groups and finally the whole class, develop solutions. After options are given, have them think through the logical consequences of each choice until they decide on the most productive. For example, if one is angry, one can hit another person; internalize the anger; tell the teacher; respond to the other student, "When you . . . , I feel . . . , because . . . . "; or have a mediated problem-solving session. Children and adolescents can easily determine which solutions and which consequences meet their needs and the needs of others. This is especially important for the ADHD student who has difficulty with impulse control. Those who are consciously taught alternative behaviors to their inappropriate responding fare much better than those who do not have the benefit of this kind of teaching.

Internalizing the rules for behavior, learning self-control, and using mental dialogue for problem-solving are the foundations for emotional maturity, good judgment and appropriate responding. They are emphasized in this approach.

SOCIAL SKILLS TRAINING

While a few ADHD students are very popular and may be class leaders, the majority of them have significant problems in social relationships. They often appear insensitive to others' feelings and needs. Their impulsive responding creates ongoing social interaction problems. Social skills training, both in the classroom and as part of a psychotherapeutic intervention program, can be quite helpful.

Some suggestions to assist you with the development of social skills in your ADHD students follow:

1) Post on the bulletin board and discuss *rules* of effective social interaction and the reasons for them.

2) Utilize stories and essays which illustrate positive human characteristics and graphically depict what happens when one is rude, selfish, mean, etc. Historically values have been taught through fables. Continue this tradition making it relevant to the beliefs you wish to impart. Many books are available for both teachers and parents to assist with this endeavor.

3) Improve writing skills and develop sensitivity by having students keep a daily diary. When incidents arise, have them address:

- What happened?

- Why did it happen?

- What were the consequences?

- How did people feel?

- How could it have been prevented?

- How can one use that situation to learn?

- What did you learn from the incident?

An additional benefit of the diary is that you learn much about the emotions and feelings of each student. You may even wish to use it to communicate encouragement and understanding through notes you write back.

4) Utilize some of the Social Skills curricula which have been developed for classroom use. Your classroom can become a mini-cosmos of life. Help students to understand that the problems they must address and resolve are, on a small scale, the very same as those being addressed by the United Nations. Help them become good citizens as well as cooperative and successful students.

5) Encourage a sense of responsibility for others among your students. Helping Johnny with his ADHD problems should become the class goal. Only when Johnny is successful should the class feel successful. Since children are by nature rule-bound and rejecting of *different* behavior, you, as the teacher, will have to establish a different *rule* and a different goal, i.e., one of helping each person become the best he can be. Help children avoid the need for *sameness for security*. Help them appreciate uniqueness and specialness by encouraging, <u>not</u> rejecting, individual differences.

INDIVIDUAL AND FAMILY COUNSELING

Individual counseling is often necessary to overcome the child or adolescent's loss of esteem, frustration and anger and to build positive coping strategies. Family counseling is also an essential adjunctive therapy in the treatment of the ADHD child. Because of their behavior, their lack of success, and their seeming indifference to discipline, ADHD children tend, over the years, to generate much psychological tension between themselves and their parents and siblings. Family counseling is necessary for understanding the disorder, learning how to manage it effectively and appropriately, and for helping the family progress from dysfunctional family interactions to healthy, positive relationships. Assistance to the family is essential to those concerned with **everyone's** ultimate well-being.

EDUCATIONAL INTERVENTION

School is one of the child's primary sources of esteem and fulfillment. Children who are not successful cannot mature into competent, productive, fully-functioning adults. Therefore, it is vital that every effort be made to ensure that the child with attention problems experiences a school environment that capitalizes on his strengths and compensates for his weaknesses. Important considerations are: appropriate grade placement, screening for learning disabilities, consideration of learning style preference, and classroom management strategies. Each of these topics is covered in detail in other sections of this handbook.

"Education is what survives when what has been learnt has been forgotten." B. F. Skinner, New Scientist 21 May 1964

MANAGING ATTENTION DISORDERS

STATEMENT OF OBJECTIVES

Fostering cooperation and discouraging competition among students may be the teacher's most important objective. Research clearly shows that happiness, productivity, and even survival are enhanced by cooperation--not competition. It, likewise, shows that children subjected to competitive environments that emphasize formal teaching and early academic pressure tend to be less creative, register more anxiety about tests, and soon lose any early academic advantage they may have gained.

TEACH COOPERATION, NOT COMPETITION

DEVELOP SOCIAL RESPONSIBILITY/PROMOTE CITIZENSHIP

While research strongly supports the values of cooperation and group accomplishment, this philosophy has not been the educational or societal orientation of our country for the last twenty years. As we have become ever more successful and more achievement-oriented, the needs of the individual have clearly usurped the collective needs of the group. Recent studies show that children today are becoming more preoccupied with themselves, less concerned about the emotional needs of others, and less emotionally attached to their families than ever before. Independence and self-reliance are perhaps the strongest values in our culture, and the emphasis on these characteristics is beginning at a younger and younger age.

There are costs, however. Children are increasingly incapable of working cooperatively. Many elementary school children are already so oriented to independence that they are unwilling or unable to work together on projects as part of a small group. They feel frustrated when asked to relinquish individual needs to meet the goals of the group.

Are we perhaps teaching children the wrong things? Are independence and self-sufficiency not best? Perhaps not. Survival of our globe has never been more dependent upon people working together to effect change and to meet challenges. Dr. Carl Thorensen, of Stanford University, after discovering Type A behaviors of impatience, anger and competitiveness in fifth grade students, notes "As human beings, we are not biologically designed to be free agents. We need to rely on each other."

There is an important lesson to be learned from the Japanese in this regard. They have the highest math and science scores in the world. Their literacy rate is also the highest. These levels of achievement were not, however, reached through a rigid system of individual achievement and an accelerated lock-step curriculum which enabled them to succeed. Rather, from kindergarten through third grade, warm and nurturing teachers, in an atmosphere of group activities and common goals, show them that getting along with others is not only a means for keeping peace in the classroom, but it is a valued end itself. It is, in fact, perhaps the most important means to the Japanese society's goals.

Lessons in how children learn can also be learned from the Japanese. The children accomplish much of their work in teams with the brighter students often helping slower ones. All children are told, "You can succeed if you persist and work hard." Scolding is not utilized, but rather praise and encouragement.

All children benefit from this emphasis on cooperation, group goals, praise and encouragement. It is perhaps easier to accomplish these objectives with non-ADHD children. While the ADHD student may be harder to teach, nevertheless, he most desperately needs the benefits of this approach to prosper. The test of each teacher's mettle may come in her ability to provide the essentials of good citizenship in a class with a difficult child.

"The prolonged education indispensable to the progress of society is not natural to mankind." Winston Churchill, MY EARLY LIFE, 1930

MANAGING ADHD IN THE CLASSROOM

Winston Churchill said, "I am always ready to learn, although I do not always like being taught." We believe that it is possible to create an environment in the classroom that will cause your students to be positive on both accounts! To create a classroom situation that will enhance learning for all your students is no small challenge, and the presence of ADHD students certainly magnifies the challenge. These students often consume inordinate amounts of your time and energy. They can easily disrupt the entire structure of your classroom, and take valuable time and attention away from their non-ADHD peers. The following guidelines are intended as ways of reducing the ADHD child's unintentional disruptions, reducing the time you must spend managing the ADHD child or adolescent, and maximizing the potential for all of your students to learn.

The following general and specific strategies have been employed in actual classrooms by teachers facing similar pressures and difficulties. While we certainly recognize that no teacher in a real classroom can implement all of these suggestions in the idealized way that they may seem to be presented here, it is important to understand that all these ideas are real classroom techniques that have been proven successful.

GENERAL STRATEGIES

1)   *Use Positive Reinforcement to Change Behavior And Motivate Students.*

The most important principle for understanding and working with ADHD children is recognizing and believing that positive, rather than negative, reinforcement must be the primary teacher tool for motivating students and changing behavior. The history of reinforcement theory in psychology has taught us that punishment does not work and that positive reinforcement is far more effective in changing and maintaining behavior. This is especially true for most ADHD children who, by second grade, have received far more negative reinforcement and punishment than the average child. Therefore, we encourage you to be positive with the ADHD students in your class. You are their hope. What you envision may well be what they become. Even when they are at their worst, try desperately not to criticize ADHD children. We understand that you may well have a mutilated tongue by the end of the day from biting it before you speak! Despite their seeming indifference, most ADHD children are deeply hurt by negative feedback. Much of their anger stems from this hurt.

When negative behaviors occur, write them down. Then establish a behavior chart with the child which is reinforced at home. Make the behavioral goals a team effort between you, the child and his parents. Children respond beautifully to structured goals which they have participated in establishing and which are consistently reinforced.

2) *Educate Your Class*

A classroom discussion on how everyone has problems can be extremely helpful. Discuss how none of us is perfect. We all have strengths and weaknesses. Some have allergies, some need glasses, some have attention problems, while still others are clumsy. The more difficulties are acknowledged, discussed and made *okay*, the more realistic and accepting children can be.

3) *Establish An Environment of Kindness and Cooperation*

One of the most effective strategies found with difficult children of any kind is making them important. Put them in positions of leadership and give them responsibilities. A program in Texas has been developed where underachieving children who are playing hookey are paid to be peer tutors for younger children. All are responding beautifully. They are attending school, they feel important and helpful, and they have positive feedback both from the younger children they are helping and their teachers. Everyone feels positive and successful--children, teachers, parents, even the governor!

4)   *Establish a Buddy System*

This is an effective strategy for teaching all children responsibility for one another as well as the personal satisfaction of giving of oneself. Children helping each other can be extremely effective. ADHD children are naturally drawn to each other and can have great friendships outside the class. Unfortunately, in class they tend to escalate each other's inappropriate behavior. Pair the ADHD child with a quiet, organized, responsible *buddy* who may, in turn, be brought out by the ADHD child. Change buddies every two to three weeks to help each child develop a relationship with every other child. Be alert to especially good fits between children and encourage those relationships even outside school.

5)   *Handle Medication With Sensitivity*

Medication is a very sensitive issue for most parents and children. It must be handled *discretely*, as most children do not want others to know they are taking medicine. This is especially true by third grade and is a major embarrassment by fifth grade. Try to avoid asking out loud, "Johnny, did you take your medicine!?" The implications are too obvious! The child may begin to resent the medication or refuse to take it altogether. He may believe that medicine is in control of his behavior and not him.

6)   *Determine Each Child's Strengths*

All children have patterns of strengths and weaknesses. Determine the ADHD child's dominant learning style and learning preferences and match your requirements with his strengths. For example, the ADHD child might be gifted in designing a visual presentation of a book he read, but have difficulty with an oral or written report. He may do a superb job as a messenger, but have difficulty leading a team. Capitalizing on strengths while working on weaker areas has a major impact on self-esteem.

ADHD children often need to be taught learning strategies that capitalize on their individual strengths. One program conducted by a learning center taught children with ADHD specific strategies such as visual notetaking, notebook organization, time management and charts for organization. At the end of six weeks, the students had increased an average of one letter grade.

7)   *Use Encouragement Generously*

Once strengths have been determined, the importance of encouragement cannot be overemphasized. From kindergarten to graduate school, all students respond positively to the encouragement of a respected teacher. Even brief words of support can have a dramatic effect. This fact is aptly demonstrated in the comments of Alfred Kazin, a Columbia University graduate, literary editor of the New Republic, and author of eight books. In reflecting upon his own educational experience in *An Apple For My Teacher*, Kazin states, "It was a relief to escape into the classes of Bird Stair, the greatest teacher I have known and the man who more than any other led me to discover myself as a writer. . . . What Bird Stair did for my reading was wonderful. What he did for my writing was--everything . . . . There came a day, an unforgettable day, when Bird Stair returned my Brahms paper to me with the dry comment: 'You have a talent for this sort of thing. I should pursue it.' Stair's terse clipped approval woke me up."

8)   *Develop a Sense of Humor*

Enjoy the children in your class. Life with an ADHD child without humor and fun is disastrous for all. Children with happy teachers learn far more than those without laughter. Developing a sense of humor may well be your saving grace--and the child's! The ability to laugh at oneself and at the foibles of children can overcome major standoffs in relationships with ADHD children. These children can be very defiant when they are threatened or feel pushed into a corner. They can, however, be like kittens when treated with respect, positive reinforcement and humor.

Humor is a powerful tool in the classroom and can be used to stimulate, motivate, illustrate and ease tensions. Exaggerate points you wish to make with humor or have students bring in a humorous item to share. Set up a bulletin board containing cartoons, photographs or humorous quotations. Another effective technique for gaining the attention of the class is to begin each class with a thought, key idea, poem, observation or even a joke. Deviate occasionally from the planned material to relate a story, personal experience, or amusing anecdote. Studies have shown that students enjoy learning with a teacher who uses humor. In fact, Carl Rogers said that a sense of humor is one of the most essential qualities for a teacher to have. Showing that you appreciate humor creates an environment of acceptance in which all children are more willing to work.

9)   *Emphasize Quality of Work - Not Quantity*

Completing classwork and homework is a source of intense frustration for ADHD children. When confronted with large amounts of written work or when turning in *all their work* is rewarded in class, many ADHD students respond by completing the work as quickly as possible without regard for its neatness or accuracy.   If they feel the workload is more than they can concentrate on or complete, they simply avoid it, refuse to do it, lose it, or *forget* it.

Increasing pressures on teachers to complete so many criterion units or so many levels of workbooks may also cause you to feel frantic. You obviously must place some emphasis on the quantity of work that is completed by your class. If, however, you identify children who are having difficulty with the volume of work, it is essential to place less emphasis on the quantity, and reinforce them enthusiastically for any assignments completed at acceptable levels of quality. This will begin the child on a cycle of encouragement and motivation that will ultimately result in his ability to handle greater and greater amounts of work.

"There are no gains without pains." Adlai Stevenson, Nomination address 1952

SPECIFIC STRATEGIES

1) *Remove Distracting Items From the Classroom*

It is important to limit the number of items in the room that are visually or auditorially stimulating. Auditory distractions are often limited by teachers who have rules against talking out or discourage drumming of fingers or pencils, jangling of keys, and other unnecessary noises. Often it is not obvious, however, the number of visual distractions that are present in the room. In fact, teachers are sometimes encouraged to make their classrooms *enriched*, which can be a highly distractible environment. Bright and interesting bulletin boards placed in view of the students, mobiles which twirl intriguingly overhead, displays of projects, aquariums, and any number of other items of high visual interest may, in fact, enrich the educational environment, but when poorly placed in the classroom, they can serve to distract even the most attentive children, much less those with attentional difficulties.

A basic rule of thumb to follow, especially for young children, is to place no visual distractions in the children's line of sight from their work areas to the areas from which the teacher actually presents material or gives directions. It is better not to have distractors at all than to display them in the midst of the visual line of sight. Research has shown that children are much less likely to look at bulletin board displays containing samples of students' work and papers during work periods than they are to look at bulletin boards containing drawings, pictures, and enrichment projects.

2) Correctly Place the ADHD Child Physically

Moving the ADHD child's desk closer to the blackboard or teacher's desk can be useful if the teacher usually presents material from near her desk and does not allow students to come to her desk while she is seated there. It can be entirely counterproductive if the practice in the classroom is to allow students to bring papers to the teacher's desk for assistance or correction. In this case, the spot closest to the teacher's desk is often the most distracting spot in the entire room and ADHD children will function poorly in this location. Locations near the pencil sharpener or with direct hall or window views are equally inappropriate. Surprisingly enough, many children with attentional problems function best toward the middle of classrooms where the primary objects in their visual and auditory fields are other children working.

For most children with attentional difficulties it is ineffective to move them to the far back or side of the room or in an individualized study compartment. This tends to isolate the children from the possibility of reward and individual attention and does not tend to encourage concentration. Also, children may interpret this as punitive, rather than as a teacher's effort to help them. Some teachers set up an *office* which is available to anyone who wants to isolate himself. Many children describe being very distracted by their classmates and welcome such self-imposed isolation. It is best to meet with your class and discuss what is distracting to them. Together you can develop a plan which is supported by all the students.

3) Increase the Distance Between Desks

Increasing the distance between desks so that the ADHD child must leave his seat or move the desk in order to touch someone else will greatly reduce the tendency to touch, kick or bother other students. A surprisingly large number of classrooms have desks so close together that it is almost impossible not to touch other students, a situation that many ADHD children find overly tempting. With large numbers of students and small classrooms this may be difficult to implement, but experience has shown that even minor changes can greatly help in overall classroom management.

4)   Teach Listening Skills

Most students with ADHD have developed poor listening habits over the years or may have never learned to listen effectively. Since they are impulsive and inattentive by nature, they have not listened for sustained periods of time. Fortunately, research has shown that listening skills can be learned. One innovative program in Nebraska with junior and senior high school students involved teaching them how to listen. Students were instructed to listen to a taped recording of the morning news broadcast and then complete worksheets on the material heard. The students then constructed the broadcast from memory as one student took notes on the blackboard. Finally, they were quizzed over the material. After six weeks the students showed a gain of twenty to forty percentage points in their ability to listen effectively.

5)   Establish Eye Contact

Children with ADHD have difficulty following directions and attending to sets of directions as a natural consequence of the brain's oversensitivity to external and internal stimuli. Because the Reticular Activating System does not limit the number of incoming stimuli, the child attends to too many stimuli at once. This interferes with his ability to focus only on the information relevant to the task at hand.

Establishing eye contact with the child makes it easier for most children to be attentive. Research strongly indicates that students whose eyes are diverted during the direction-giving process are the ones least likely to recall and follow the instructions given. If you give directions while facing away from the students, writing on the blackboard, looking down at your desk or from the back of the room, it may aggravate the problem.

Asking students to look at you before giving the instructions and placing yourself so that students have a direct view of your face, especially your mouth, will maximize the likelihood that students will follow directions.

Another very effective technique, especially in the elementary grades, is to have the entire class repeat oral instruction sentence-by-sentence verbatim. Even though this is time-consuming, it greatly increases their attention to the instructions and benefits the students' auditory memory and sequencing skills as well. If the directions are printed on written worksheets, you may wish to have various children read the directions aloud for each worksheet before written work begins.

6) *Vary Voice Tone and Inflection*

Research does not indicate that louder or softer tones per se increase attention to instructions, but rather that varying the tone is the critical factor. It is effective to give oral instructions twice, changing the volume between presentations. Emphasizing the most important parts of the instruction, such as the worksheet title, page number, or problem numbers, in louder tones than the rest of the instructions will also help. It is equally useful occasionally to ask your students to listen very carefully and then give instructions in soft tones. While adults depend heavily on changes in a speaker's voice tone and facial expression to maintain their interest, children depend much more heavily still on these cues.

Experience has shown that sitting while speaking seems to create a more monotone delivery. Move around the room as you speak and use body gestures to animate and emphasize your words. Many teachers have found it helpful to periodically record or videotape their lessons. Seeing or hearing yourself as your students do may prove very revealing.

7) *Combine Sight, Sound and Motor Cues*

Many ADHD children have problems with visual memory or auditory discrimination and, therefore, perform best with a combination of oral and written directions. Many learn best by doing. It is important to try to give as much information as possible in every modality. Use colored chalk to underline key words. Use rhythm and music to learn rote facts. Teach history through drama. Learn science in the school yard.

When a child is consistently having trouble understanding you, establish a discrete signal so that he can let you know when he is having difficulty with directions and explanations. Children are very creative in developing signals. They enjoy your interest and usually disrupt with questions much less frequently.

8) *Emphasize With Color*

Color added to highlight important parts of tasks can greatly help the ADHD child pay attention. One study conducted by researchers at Purdue University and Ball State University found that ADHD children performed better when color was used to emphasize relevant details. It is interesting, however, that when color was used randomly just to increase the attractiveness of the tasks, it became distracting and interfered with the children's performance. Highlighting important parts of directions or underlining key words in a math problem assists students in focusing on the major information. Doing this for them initially and then teaching them how to identify these key words may ultimately help students in older grades more than any other skill.

9) *Create Learning Partners*

Time spent at the desk each day doing independent written work is often the most difficult time of the day for many ADHD children. This is when disruptive behavior and inattention are most likely to occur or **to** be the most severe. Pairing the ADHD child with a *Partner* who has good on-**task** behavior results in peer encouragement to be on-task and attentive. Many teachers have found this to be more effective than teacher correction and it is frequently perceived to be less negative by the child. It may also benefit the hypoactive ADHD child to pair him with an enthusiastic, outgoing, high-energy child. While these *Partner* systems can sometimes require considerable adjustment and fine-tuning before they are perfected for each individual classroom, the rewards for students and teachers can be enormous.

10) Keep Individual Work Periods Short

When individual work is to be done in the classroom, it is most effective to provide short and well-structured time units for its completion. Independent written work periods for early primary students should be kept to a maximum of fifteen or twenty minutes. All worksheets for the day should not be assigned at the beginning of the day but rather should be assigned one or two at a time, followed by a break for other activities. A major problem we are seeing with all children is that they are being required to sit and do seat work for long periods without breaks. They are also getting little physical exercise. These two practices alone may be greatly increasing the number of children with attentional problems.

11) Do Not Use Timers

Placing a timer on the desk of a slow or unproductive worker usually worsens the overall situation and sometimes produces serious complications. The noise of the timer is a strong auditory distractor and, for most slow workers, the whole process is seen as a negative reinforcer. Even if children increase the amount of work completed, the quality of their handwriting and accuracy often suffers.

Unfortunately, only constant monitoring and positive encouragement from the teacher, without undue emphasis on the quantity of work produced, actually improves the problem. Helping the child divide the work so he can attack it in small pieces also helps.

12) Allow For Physical Movement

Even adults lose their ability to concentrate if they remain immobile for long periods of time. Body movement, *kinesthesis,* is a critical component of our learning and is especially important in childhood. Most preschool programs recognize this need and allow considerable movement about the room and time for free play. However, in many first grades children are expected to remain seated without appreciable body movement for quite long periods, and by the middle elementary years students are expected to remain in their desks for forty-five or fifty-minute periods without a break for physical movement. This type of classroom setting brings out the very worst in high-activity ADHD children since their actual body metabolism demands movement and the expenditure of more energy than their age peers.

One dedicated fifth grade teacher discovered that one of her very hyperactive students shared her love of jogging. She began inviting him to join her during her lunch-time jogs around the school grounds. She discovered, much to her delight, that his ability to pay attention increased significantly for the remainder of the school day.

Underactive, or hypoactive, children are equally poorly served because long periods of being seated increase their inattention and daydreaming and sometimes actually lead them to fall asleep.

Physical activity and learning are not incompatible. In fact, physical activity can be an essential part of academic learning. It is not necessary to have children run around the school, as in the extreme example given above. Even the simple act of standing and sitting several times within a class period provides enough physical movement to release significant energy for the hyperactive child and prevents the hypoactive child from becoming entirely tuned out. There are several strategies to incorporate movement that can be used successfully in the classroom. These include:

- Auditory drills with primary children. The teacher calls out a letter, or group of letters, and the students respond by giving the sound that the letter or letters produce. The children are standing and the teacher is walking around the room.

- Random counting drills where the students count by ones, or twos, or fives, with the teacher pointing to the student who should respond next, again standing.

- With older students, math fact drills can be conducted standing beside desks.

- With high school students, standing oral drills where the teacher states a fact to be learned and the students recite in unison. This can be easily applied to chemistry formulas, history facts, etc.

- Have students act out parts of characters, carry out projects, build things or interview people.

Restructuring the classroom so that there is a physical outlet for the ADHD child's energy can eliminate many of his behavioral disruptions. Experience has shown that ADHD students function least effectively and produce the most disruptions in those classrooms that place the highest level of demands on them for sitting still.

13)   *Help Him Eliminate Careless Errors In Math*

Two helpful strategies for eliminating many careless errors on math problems are:

1) Have the child circle the sign to insure that he pays attention to it. He is less likely to multiply if he has just circled the sign for division.

2) Using graph paper will help ADHD children who have trouble keeping figures aligned. It should be paper with large graphs or blocks. (Several examples are included in the Appendix).

14) *Play Classical Music*

Playing classical or baroque music during study periods may also help reduce distractions. This is the music advocated by proponents of Superlearning. The steady beat alerts the Reticular System and focuses the child. Auditorially distracted children may, however, find it a problem. Check with your students to see if it is helpful.

White noise machines which produce very steady, consistent sound also help the child to focus. Many government buildings are equipped with these to increase efficiency.

15) *Help Reduce The Frustration Of Writing*

Writing is a problem for approximately eighty percent of ADHD children. It produces the most frustration and greatest sense of failure from preschool to college. Many ADHD children can verbalize beautifully, but will not invest the exorbitant and exhausting amount of energy necessary to control their attention and impulsivity long enough to complete lengthy written tasks. They will do just about *anything* to avoid this defeat.

Be creative and do not force your students to go to such lengths. Decide what is essential and eliminate what is unnecessary. If a visual presentation will do as well as a written composition, not only allow it, but encourage it. Photocopying vocabulary words may help a child learn them just as effectively as writing each word in a sentence. Typing and word processing can be used as early as first grade, and the use of a dictaphone and transcriber is easily mastered by third and fourth grades. Determine with the ADHD child in your classroom a creative means of meeting your educational goals. When writing is necessary, emphasize careful, neat work without excessive recopying and staying in from recess. Both overactive and underactive children desperately need these physical-energy and tension-release breaks.

In the technical world of the '90's, it is not necessary for people to be handicapped by poor handwriting skills. Computers will be a major part of the teaching process in the future. Many ADHD children enjoy the computer and can learn to print papers at a very early age.

Implementing some or several of these recommendations may not be easy. In fact, considerable time and effort is often needed to accomplish these goals. However, over the years hundreds of teachers have expressed feelings of frustration and inadequacy in dealing with these children. It is hoped that these suggestions for restructuring or modifying your classroom might turn these frustrations into feelings of accomplishment and satisfaction. While you may not often know immediately the effect you have had on an ADHD child, your care and concern will undoubtedly have a tremendous impact. The results obtained are well worth the energy invested.

"There is always one moment in childhood when the door opens and lets in the future." Graham Greene, THE POWER AND THE GLORY 1940

TEACHER'S SUCCESS STORY

As the Director of a preschool I had experienced the many joys and occasional frustrations of guiding preschoolers and teachers. During the two years I had been director, I had felt very confident of my administrative ability. My biggest problem was my own young son who was enrolled in my preschool. He seemed forever involved in an altercation with a friend, a scrape with a peer, or an unthinking act of defiance. His teachers were patient and caring, but I could sense their frustration. I asked them many times to advise me of his progress and to report any problems or concerns. Whether from fear of jeopardizing their relationship with me or from their natural inclination to cope rather than confront a parent, they did not.

My husband and I also felt helpless and overwhelmed at times by Robert's determination, persistence and noncompliance with our expectations. While we prided ourselves on being loving, consistent parents who could help him overcome these problems, it was impossible to be caring and consistent at *all* times with a child on whom raised voices, spankings and other forms of discipline had little effect.

The kindergarten episodes had not been our first cause for concern. We knew Robert would be a challenge from the moment he began swimming laps in my stomach. In retrospect, it seemed as if his entire life had been building to this point. An episode at school one day forced me into facing his difficulties head on. While the behavior itself was not a major problem, the reaction of the parents of the children involved was. I learned very quickly how anger and blame can be aroused when parents feel any harm can come to their child. I now know that for parents and teachers the other half of dealing with an ADHD child's problems is dealing with the parents of the children he may in some way be threatening.

We saw a psychologist and our son was diagnosed as having ADHD. We began using behavior management programs and also established a responsibility program at home. We also started using the Thinking Chair. This strategy enabled us to exercise control over Robert for the first time. A positive reinforcement system was also introduced. Our son loved collecting chips for his good behavior at school and more chips for his good behavior and responsibilities at home. While he used the chips to purchase things he wanted, it was clear that the real value of the chip was its psychological value. To him it said, "You are a good and a capable child." Hugs and praises given with the chips solidified that intrinsic sense of self-worth. As Robert learned self-control and became more confident, the necessity of the Thinking Chair declined dramatically. We soon found positive incentives almost sufficient.

We continued our concrete reinforcement program for specific behaviors through first grade. While he did well, it became increasingly apparent that psychological and behavioral interventions were not quite enough. Robert's pediatrician put him on medication in January. Robert had a great year afterwards and finished first grade both confidently and successfully.

After my experiences with Robert, we implemented the programs outlined in this handbook throughout our preschool. The difference has been considerable. The children love the praise and encouragement and a problem behavior goes on the "Daily Progress Report" to parents until successfully resolved. Troublesome misbehaviors do not go unaddressed but, rather, become goals for the child, his parents, the teacher, and often goals for the entire class.

While I would not wish difficulties for anyone, I am grateful that the incident alerted me to ADHD. My understanding has enabled me to help my fellow teachers deal more effectively with ADHD children and their parents. We now recognize those children with attentional disorders and immediately go into action to help them overcome any problems. We have learned how to work on our students' weaker areas and emphasize their positive ones. The happy result has been that in our classrooms, and our school in general, we now have considerably more *attention without tension!*

REFERENCES

1. American Psychiatric Association: *Diagnostic and Statistical Manual of Mental Disorders (Fourth Edition)*. Washington, D.C., American Psychiatric Association, 1994, pp. 78-84.

2. American Psychiatric Association: *Diagnostic and Statistical Manual of Mental Disorders (Third Edition - Revised - DSM III-R)*. Washington, D.C., American Psychiatric Association, 1987, pp. 52-53, 95.

3. Bayles, Fred and McCartney, Scott: Scientology Group Wages War Against Ritalin "Baby Druggies". *Los Angeles Herald Examiner*, April 4, 1988.

4. Bredekamp, Sue and Shepard, Lorrie: How to Best Protect Children from Inappropriate School Expectations, Practices and Policies. *Young Children*, March, 1989, pp. 14-24.

5. Butler, K.G.: *Language Disorders in Children*, Austin, Texas: PRO-ED, 1986.

6. Citizens Commission on Human Rights (Sponsored by Church of Scientology): How Psychiatry is Making Drug Addicts Out of America's School Children. *CCHR Information Letter #1*, Los Angeles, 1987, pp. 1-14.

7. Copeland, Edna D.: *Developing Your Child's Potential through Knowledge, Discipline and Encouragement*. (Audio program) Confident, Capable, Cooperative Children Series. Atlanta, 3 C's of Childhood, Inc., 1988.

8. Copeland, Edna D.: *Medications for Attention Disorders (ADHD/ADD) and Related Medical Problems*. Plantation, FL: Specialty Press, Inc., 1995.

9. Copeland, Edna D.: *The Joy of a Job Well Done*. (Audio Program) Confident, Capable, Cooperative Children Series. Atlanta, 3 C's of Childhood, Inc., 1988.

10. Copeland, Edna D. and Love, Valerie: *Attention, Please! A Comprehensive Guide for Successfully Parenting Children with Attention Disorders and Hyperactivity (ADHD/ADD)*. Plantation, FL: Specialty Press, Inc., 1995.

11. Copps, Stephen C.: *The Attending Physician - Attention Deficit Disorders: A Guide for Pediatricians and Family Physicians*. Plantation, FL: Specialty Press, Inc., 1995.

12. Cowart, Virginia S.: The Ritalin Controversy: What's Made This Drug's Opponents Hyperactive? *Journal of the American Medical Association*, 1988, vol. 259, no. 17, pp. 2521-2524.

13. Davis, Michael K.:   Preparing Teachers for Developmentally Appropriate Kindergarten Classrooms. *Dimensions*, April, 1989.

14. Forster, Patricia, and Doyle, Beverly A.: Teaching Listening Skills to Students with Attention Deficit Disorders. *Teaching Exceptional Children*, 1989, Winter, pp. 20-22.

15. Golden, Gerald S., M.D.: The Relationship Between Stimulant Medication and Tics. *Pediatric Annals*, 1988, vol. 17, no. 6, pp. 405-408.

16. Healy, Jane M., Ph.D.: *Your Child's Growing Mind.* Garden City, Doubleday, 1987.

17. Hirsch-Pasek, Kathy and Marion Hyson, Leslie Pescorla and Jessica Cone: *Hurrying Children.   How does it affect their academic, social, creative and emotional development?* Presented at the Biennial Meeting for the Society for Research in Child Development in Kansas City, Missouri, April 27-30, 1989.

18. Hunsaker, Johanna S.: It's No Joke: Using Humor in the Classroom. *Clearing House*, 1988, vol. 61, pp. 285-286.

19. Hunt, Robert D., M.D.: Clonidine and Treatment of ADHD. *The Psychiatric Times*, 1988, September, pp. 10-12.

20. Ilg, Frances L. and Louise Bates Ames and Jacqueline Haines and Glyde Gillespie: *School Readiness.* New York, Harper & Row, 1978.

21. Interagency Committee on Learning Disabilities: *Learning Disabilities: A Report to the U.S. Congress.* Washington, D.C., Government Printing Office, 1987, pp. 194-217.

22. Kazin, Alfred: Teachers and Two Particular Teachers. In Rubin, Louis D. (Ed.): *An Apple For My Teacher.* Chapel Hill, Algonquin Books of Chapel Hill, 1987.

23. Kinsbourne, Marcel and Caplan, Paula J.: *Children's Learning and Attention Problems.* Boston, Little, Brown & Co., 1979.

24. Klorman, Rafael, Ph.D., Coons, Hilary W., Ph.D., and Borgstedt, Agneta D., M.D.: Effects of Methylphenidate on Adolescents With a Childhood History of Attention Deficit Disorder: I. Clinical Findings. *Journal of the American Academy of Child and Adolescent Psychiatry*, 1987, vol. 26, no. 3, pp. 363-367.

25. Kohn, Alfie: Suffer the Restless Children. *The Atlantic Monthly*, November, 1989, pp. 90-100.

26.   Lou, Hans C., Henriksen, L., Bruhn, P., Borner, H., and Nielsen, J.B.: Striated Dysfunction in Attention Deficit and Hyperkinetic Disorder. *Archives of Neurology*, 1989, vol. 46, pp. 48-52.

27.   Masland, Richard L. and Mary L. Masland: *Prevention of Reading Failure*. York Press: Parkton, Maryland, 1988.

28.   Meents, Cassandra K.: Attention Deficit Disorder: A Review of Literature. *Psychology in the Schools*, 1989, vol. 26, pp. 168-177.

29.   Partin, Ronald L.: Fifteen Guidelines for Developing Attention-Holding Lessons. *Middle School Journal*, 1987, February, pp. 12-13.

30.   Pepper, Frank S.: *The Wit and Wisdom of the Twentieth Century*. New York, Peter Bedrick Books, 1987.

31.   Schrag, P., and Divoky, D.: *The Myth of the Hyperactive Child*. New York, Pantheon Books, 1970.

32.   Shaywitz, Sally E., and Shawywitz, Bennett A.: Attention Deficit Disorder: Current Perspectives. In J. Kavanaugh and T. Truss, Jr. (Eds.), *Learning Disabilities: Proceedings of the National Conference* (1987). Parkton, York Press, 1988, 369-523.

33.   Still, George F.: The Coulstonian Lectures on Some Abnormal Physical Conditions in Children. *Lancet*, Vol. 1, 1902, pp. 1008-1012.

34.   Thorensen, Carl: The Young and the Selfish. Reported in *Self*, September, 1989, p. 228.

35.   Uphoff, James K. and Gilmore, June: Local Research Ties Suicides to Early School Entrance Studies. *Dayton Daily News*, July 26, 1984.

36.   Uphoff, James K. and Gilmore, June: Pupil Age at School Entrance -How Many are Ready for Success? *Young Children*, January, 1986.

37.   U.S. Department of Health and Human Services. Food and Drug Administration. Paul Leber, Rockville, Maryland. Letter to Ciba-Geigy Corporation, May 12, 1988.

38.   U.S. Office of Child Development: *Report of the 1971 Conference on the Use of Stimulant Drugs in the Treatment of Behaviorally Disturbed Young School Children*. Washington, D.C., Government Printing Office, 1971, pp. 4-8.

39.   Weaver, Richard L., Cotrell, Howard W.: Ten Specific Techniques for Developing Humor in the Classroom. *Education*, 1987, vol. 108, pp. 167-179.

40.   Weisberg, Lynne W., and Greenberg, R.: *When Acting Out Isn't Acting*. PIA Press, Washington, 1988.

41.   Weiss, Gabrielle & Hechtman, Lily Trokenberg: *Hyperactive Children Grown Up*. New York, The Guilford Press, 1986.

42.   White, Merry: *The Japanese Educational Challenge*. New York, MacMillan, 1989.

43.   Wolk, Ronald A.: Profession in Waiting. *Teacher Magazine*, April, 1990, p. 3.

44.   Zametkin, Alan J., M.D., Borcherding, Breck G., M.D.: The Neuropharmacology of Attention-Deficit Hyperactivity Disorder. *Annual Review of Medicine*, 1989, vol. 40, pp. 447-451.

45.   Zametkin, Alan J., et al.: Cerebral Glucose Metabolism in Adults with Hyperactivity of Childhood Onset. *New England Journal of Medicine*, 1990, vol. 323, pp. 1361-1366.

46.   Ziv, Avgner: Teaching and Learning with Humor: Experiment and Replication. *Journal of Experimental Education*, 1988, vol. 57, pp. 5-15.

APPENDIX OF FORMS

IDENTIFICATION AND GOAL-SETTING

PROBLEM SOLVING ASSESSMENT

Student:_____

A. Academic Areas of Concern:

       <u>Example: Poor Memory</u>   Ex. <u>Can't follow 3-step direction</u>
1. _____ Ex. _____
2. _____ Ex. _____
3. _____ Ex. _____
4. _____ Ex. _____
5. _____ Ex. _____

B. Behaviors of Concern:

       <u>Example: Disorganized</u>   Ex. <u>Loses homework & assignments</u>
1. _____ Ex. _____
2. _____ Ex. _____
3. _____ Ex. _____
4. _____ Ex. _____
5. _____ Ex. _____

C. Student's Strengths/Assets

Example: Great sense of humor - excellent athlete.

1. _____
2. _____
3. _____
4. _____
5. _____

D. Student's Weak Points

Example: Lack of confidence.

1. _____
2. _____
3. _____
4. _____
5. _____
6. _____

MY STUDENT'S BEHAVIOR

Negative Behaviors

	Date	Time	What Happened	Possible Goal of Behavior	My Reaction
1.	___	___	_____	_____	_____
2.	___	___	_____	_____	_____
3.	___	___	_____	_____	_____
4.	___	___	_____	_____	_____
5.	___	___	_____	_____	_____
6.	___	___	_____	_____	_____

Positive Behaviors

	Date	Time	What Happened	Possible Goal of Behavior	My Reaction
1.	___	___	_____	_____	_____
2.	___	___	_____	_____	_____
3.	___	___	_____	_____	_____
4.	___	___	_____	_____	_____
5.	___	___	_____	_____	_____
6.	___	___	_____	_____	_____

CHILD/ADOLESCENT'S ASSESSMENT
OF HOME AND SCHOOL

A. School

    (1) Tell me about school.

    (2) What do you like?

    (3) What do you dislike?

    (4) Any problems?

    (5) What changes would make things better at school?

    (6) How would you solve problems?

B. Home

Things I like:

Things I don't like:

Things I feel are fair:

Things I feel are unfair:

What changes would make things better at home?

Ways To Solve The Problems:

Home:

School:

OVERALL SUMMARY

FOR

MEETING WITH TEACHER, CHILD/ADOLESCENT

AND PARENTS

Rank   I.   **PROBLEMS**

                A. Academic

                B. Social/Emotional/Behavioral

Rank   II.   **STRENGTHS**

                A. Academic

                B. Social/Emotional/Behavioral

Rank   III.   **GOALS**

                A. Academic

                B. Social/Emotional/Behavioral

TWO-WEEK GOALS

AGREED UPON BY TEACHER AND STUDENT

I. ACADEMIC

    a) _____

    b) _____

    c) _____

II. ORGANIZATIONAL

    a) _____

    b) _____

    c) _____

III. BEHAVIORAL

    a) _____

    b) _____

    c) _____

ACADEMICS SUMMARY
FOR MEETING WITH TEACHER,
CHILD/ADOLESCENT AND PARENTS

1) Subject: _____

   Current Grade: _____

   Problem Areas: _____

   Strengths: _____

2) Subject: _____

   Current Grade: _____

   Problem Areas: _____

   Strengths: _____

3) Subject: _____

   Current Grade: _____

   Problem Areas: _____

   Strengths: _____

4) Subject: _____

   Current Grade: _____

   Problem Areas: _____

   Strengths: _____

5) Subject: _____

   Current Grade: _____

   Problem Areas: _____

   Strengths: _____

6) P.E., Art & Music _____

   _____

   _____

   _____

LETTER TO PARENTS

Dear _____:

      (Parents)

      As I mentioned in our phone conversation, _____is having difficulty in school. I am especially concerned about the following:

ACADEMICS

    1. _____
    2. _____
    3. _____

_____also has strengths academically which include _____
_____

BEHAVIOR

    1. _____
    2. _____

_____and I have met and have tried to overcome these difficulties. At this time, I feel your involvement and assistance is necessary.

      To make our meeting most productive, I am doing the following and would appreciate your doing the same at home.

1) Please list the behaviors which concern you and when they occur on the enclosed form. Also note positive behaviors and strengths.
2) Please complete the Symptom Checklists enclosed (Preschool or Elementary). Also complete the Symptom Checklist for Attention Deficit Disorders (Preschool - College).
3) Please comment on _____'s academics as you see them. Since you work with him at home, you may observe things of which I am unaware.

      I appreciate your assistance immensely. While truly understanding _____'s problems may take some extra time, in the long run it will save both your time and energy and mine. More importantly, we can save him much frustration and failure by addressing his difficulties now. I do appreciate your extra time and effort and know that together we can define _____'s problems and strengths and then efficiently and effectively provide solutions.

      I look forward to meeting with you on _____, _____, at _____.

                           Day   Date   Time

                           Sincerely,

                           Teacher

LETTER TO PROFESSIONAL

Dear _____:

Mr./Mrs. _____have advised me that they are having _____
Student

evaluated/treated by you. With their permission, I am enclosing copies of behavior checklists, completed by both the parents and me, as well as academic data, and a summary of my intervention efforts with _____. I hope this information is helpful to you.

At _____Elementary School, we believe strongly in a TEAM approach in treating children who are having difficulties in school. I shall be happy to speak with you or be of any assistance possible in the evaluation and treatment process. As a team, I feel confident we can help _____.

I look forward to hearing from you.

Sincerely,

_____
Teacher

Phone No. (W)

Enclosures: Copy of Parental Consent
Student Information

WRITTEN CONSENT

TO: _____

_____, my child's teacher, has permission to release academic, behavioral and social/emotional data on my child to you and to discuss his/her difficulties and/or progress with you.

_____ (Parent)

_____ (Address)

(___)_____ (Phone No.)

Child: _____

School: _____

Phone No.: (___)_____

Southeastern Psychological INSTITUTE

PRESCHOOL CHECK UP

A SYMPTOM CHECKLIST FOR DEVELOPMENTAL DISABILITIES

Edna D. Copeland, Ph.D., Director
Child/Clinical Psychologist

Southeastern Psychological Institute
P.O. Box 12389
Atlanta, Georgia 30355-2389
(404) 256-4333

Dedicated to Prevention through Early Intervention SM
© Copyright, Edna D. Copeland Ph.D., 1984, 1987

II. HEARING/AUDITORY PERCEPTION/AUDITORY PROCESSING

____ 1. Does your child have trouble remembering things?

____ 2. Does your child seem to "tune-out" or day-dream at times?

____ 3. Was your child's speech late or abnormal in any way?

____ 4. Did your child have chronic ear infections during any time from birth to age 6?

____ 5. Was your child late in learning his/her colors, numbers or alphabet?

____ 6. Does your child continue to have speech substitutions, e.g. "f" for "th", ("free" for "three"), "w" for "l", ("bawoon" for "balloon"), etc.

____ 7. Do other people have difficulty understanding your child's speech?

____ 8. Do you often have to repeat directions for your child?

____ 9. Does it seem that your child pays very little attention to you?

____ 10. Is your child unable to modulate his/her voice, i.e, speak softly when in quiet situations and louder when needed to be heard?

____ 11. Does your child talk very loudly, even during normal conversations?

____ 12. When called from another room, does your child frequently not respond?

____ 13. Does your child frequently turn the same ear in the direction of sound?

____ 14. Does your child complain that his ears hurt or ring?

____ 15. Is there a history of hearing or auditory problems in your family?

III. VISION/VISUAL PERCEPTION/VISUAL PROCESSING/VISUAL-MOTOR SKILLS

____ 1. Does your child have little interest in puzzles, legos, and visual toys?

____ 2. Did your child have difficulty learning to recognize colors, shapes, letters and numbers?

____ 3. Does your child confuse letters, numbers, shapes or words which are similar?

____ 4. Are your child's drawings immature and lacking in detail?

____ 5. Does your child have difficulty putting toys or games together?

____ 6. Does your child have trouble producing letters, numbers and words on demand even though he can recognize them?

____ 7. Does your child have difficulty recognizing letters, numbers, shapes, words or objects if parts are missing?

____ 8. Does/did your child reverse letters (b/d), numbers (6/9), or words (saw/was)?

____ 9. Did your child have difficulty learning right and left?

____ 10. Does your child get lost easily or seem confused about directions?

____ 11. Does your child have a poor concept of time?

____ 12. Are your child's verbal abilities much better than written expression? Does he/she dislike writing?

____ 13. Does your child have difficulty coloring within lines or writing as well as his peers?

____ 14. Does your child avoid games or activities involving catching or throwing a ball?

____ 15. Does your child squint when looking at the board or far away objects?

IV. MEDICAL

____ 1. Does your child get frequent headaches?

____ 2. Is your child often tired?

____ 3. Did your child have difficulty establishing bowel and bladder control?

____ 4. Does your child still have relapses in bowel or bladder control either day or night?

____ 5. Does your child have a poor appetite?

____ 6. Does your child have a history of anemia of any type?

____ 7. Is your child irritable before and/or shortly after meals?

____ 8. Does your child crave sweets?

____ 9. Was your child colicky as an infant?

____ 10. Was your child an unusually cranky baby?

____ 11. Was your child an unusually passive baby?

____ 12. Does your child have a history of allergies?

____ 13. Is there a history of allergies in the family?

Name of Child: _____

Date: _____

Completed by: _____

NEED FOR EARLY RECOGNITION OF DEVELOPMENTAL PROBLEMS IN PRESCHOOLERS

The years from 4 through 6 are critical years in the intellectual, visual-motor, psycholinguistic and personality development of the child. Although often treated as an in-between age, this age period constitutes a well-defined landmark in the young child's mental, language, visual, perceptual and motor development. It is also the period when he/she is exposed for the first time to some type of formal education and is brought into wider social contacts with children of his/her own age. By age 4 a child's intellectual, psycholinguistic, visual-motor and personality characteristics are developed sufficiently well to determine deviations, both positively and negatively. By age 5 almost every precursor of learning, attention and behavior problems is apparent. Likewise, giftedness and accelerated capabilities are also easily recognized. All children have individual patterns of relative assets and weaknesses. It is important to understand these even in the child without special needs or gifts so that his assets can be realized to the fullest.

Approximately 27% of the preschool population has been described as "At Risk" for Developmental Disabilities. For preventive reasons, it appears expedient to recognize developmental delays in children between the ages of 4½ to 6. Careful evaluation, planning and remediation can preclude or minimize, as much as possible, learning, attention, and behavior disorders at the elementary school level. Likewise, plans can be made to provide for the gifted or talented child's special needs. Relatively individualized programs for all children can be established to capitalize upon their assets.

The **SOUTHEASTERN PSYCHOLOGICAL INSTITUTE** is especially concerned with identifying and remediating Developmental Disabilities. It is far easier to treat and remediate difficulties at an early age before children have experienced failure, frustration and subsequent academic, social, and emotional problems.

The Symptom Checklist for Developmental Disabilities was developed by Dr. Edna D. Copeland after 15 years of clinical practice to help parents and teachers determine whether their children or the children they teach have Developmental Disabilities.

SYMPTOM CHECKLIST

This checklist was developed from the experience of many specialists in the fields which comprise Developmental Disabilities. The questions asked are warning signals of conditions which may interfere with your child's academic, emotional and social adjustment now and in the future.

If you answer "Yes" to as many as 20% of the questions, it may mean that your child has a Developmental Disability. A Developmental Disability does *not* mean that a child is lacking in intelligence or capability. Rather, it means that a child might have difficulty achieving academically and/or socially at his/her level of ability.

Directions: Place a checkmark (✓) by those questions to which your answer is "Yes". Do not mark questions to which you answer "No".

SYMPTOM CHECKLIST FOR DEVELOPMENTAL DISABILITIES

I. ATTENTION / CONCENTRATION / IMPULSE CONTROL / BEHAVIOR

1. Does your child interrupt frequently?
2. Is your child easily distracted?
3. Is your child up and down frequently during meals?
4. Is your child's work often sloppy although it can be neat if he/she really tries?
5. Does your child move from activity to activity without settling down to any one thing for long?
6. Is there inconsistency in your child's performance, i.e., one day he/she performs a task well; the next day, he/she performs the same task poorly?
7. Does your child have difficulty playing alone?
8. Was your child not cuddly as an infant?
9. Did your child require little sleep as an infant?
10. Is your child more demanding than other children?
11. Is punishment ineffective with your child?
12. Is your child rejected by peers and/or adults?
13. Is your child always better in a one-to-one situation?
14. Is your child beginning to think of himself as "mean" or "dumb"?
15. Does you child "fidget" a lot?
16. Does your child often fail to finish things he/she starts?
17. Does your child have difficulty concentrating on tasks requiring sustained attention?
18. Is your child excitable and impulsive?
19. Does your child deny mistakes or blame others?
20. Is your child immature for his/her age?
21. Does your child's mood change quickly and drastically?
22. Does your child have temper tantrums?
23. Is your child more active than his/her peers?
24. Does your child become frustrated easily?
25. Does your child have poor self-control?
26. Is your child extremely daring?
27. Is your child a discipline problem?
28. Does your child find it necessary to touch everything he/she sees?
29. Does your child bother other children — either by touching them or intruding into their activities and conversations?
30. Does your child have difficulty waiting his turn in games or group situations?
31. Do birthday parties and situations with a lot of stimulation cause your child to become overly excited and lose control?
32. Is your child consistently less active than other children?
33. Is your child afraid of heights?
34. Does your child bully other children?
35. Is your child purposely destructive or hurtful of others?

131

Southeastern Psychological INSTITUTE

A CHECK UP
FOR
ELEMENTARY SCHOOL CHILDREN

A SYMPTOM CHECKLIST FOR BEHAVIORAL, ATTENTIONAL, LEARNING AND EMOTIONAL DIFFICULTIES

by

Edna D. Copeland, Ph.D.
Child / Clinical Psychologist

Southeastern Psychological Institute
P.O. Box 12389
Atlanta, Georgia 30355-2389
(404) 256-4333

Dedicated to Prevention through Early Intervention

© Copyright, Edna D. Copeland, Ph.D., 1984, 1987

---

6. Does your child continue to have speech substitutions, e.g., "f" for "th" ("free" for "three") "w" for "l" ("bawoon" for "balloon"), etc?
7. Do other people have difficulty understanding your child's speech?
8. Do you often have to repeat directions for your child?
9. Does it seem that your child pays very little attention to you?
10. Is your child unable to modulate his/her voice, i.e., speak softly when in quiet situations and louder when needed to be heard?
11. Does your child talk very loudly, even during normal conversations?
12. When called from another room, does your child frequently not respond?
13. Does your child frequently turn the same ear in the direction of sound?
14. Does your child complain that his ears hurt or ring?
15. Is there a history of hearing or auditory problems in your family?

IV. VISION/VISUAL PERCEPTION/ VISUAL PROCESSING/VISUAL-MOTOR SKILLS

1. Does your child have little interest in puzzles, legos, and visual toys?
2. Did your child have difficulty learning to recognize colors, shapes, letters and numbers?
3. Does your child confuse letters, numbers, shapes or words which are similar?
4. Are your child's drawings immature and lacking in detail?
5. Does your child have difficulty putting toys or games together?
6. Does your child have trouble producing letters, numbers and words on demand even though he can recognize them?

---

7. Does your child have difficulty recognizing letters, numbers, shapes, words or objects if parts are missing?
8. Does/did your child reverse letters (b/d), numbers (6/9), or words (saw/was)?
9. Did your child have difficulty learning right and left?
10. Does your child get lost easily or seem confused about directions?
11. Does your child have a poor concept of time?
12. Are your child's verbal abilities much better than written expression? Does he/she dislike writing?
13. Does your child have difficulty coloring within lines or writing as well as his peers?
14. Does your child avoid games or activities involving catching or throwing a ball?
15. Does your child squint when looking at the board or far away objects?

V. ACADEMIC/ACHIEVEMENT

1. Is your child's academic achievement below the level you had expected based on ability? Do the teachers say, "He/she is not working up to potential?"
2. Is your child's daily performance in school inconsistent, remembering things he/she has learned one day and not the next?
3. Is your child having difficulty reading or understanding what he/she reads?
4. Does your child seem afraid or embarrassed to ask questions at school?
5. Does your child follow academic directions poorly?
6. Does your child dislike school?
7. Does your child have difficulty with math but enjoy reading and spelling?
8. Does your child have difficulty completing class assignments within the allotted time?
9. Has your child's teacher expressed concern about any area of academic performance?
10. Has your child had difficulty adjusting to classroom routine and discipline?

VI. MEDICAL

1. Does your child get frequent headaches and/or stomachaches?
2. Is your child always tired?
3. Did your child have difficulty establishing bowel and bladder control?
4. Does your child still have relapses in bowel or bladder control either day or night?
5. Does your child have a poor appetite?
6. Does your child have a history of anemia of any type?
7. Is your child irritable before and/or shortly after meals?
8. Does your child crave sweets?
9. Was your child colicky as an infant?
10. Was your child an unusually cranky baby?
11. Was your child an unusually passive baby?
12. Does your child have a history of allergies?
13. Is there a history of allergies in the family?

Name of Child: _____

Date: _____

Completed by: _____

PREVENTION OF LEARNING, BEHAVIOR AND EMOTIONAL DISORDERS THROUGH EARLY IDENTIFICATION, REMEDIATION, TREATMENT AND EDUCATION.

It is becoming increasingly apparent that school failure, behavioral problems, juvenile delinquency, drug and alcohol abuse, and problems of social and work adjustment in adolescents and adults have their origins very early in life. Some estimate that as many as 70% of both the learning and emotional problems encountered in adolescents and adults began in unrecognized problems of childhood. Many of these difficulties can be detected by age 6, and younger, as developmental disabilities. These disabilities include learning disorders; communicative disorders; visual-perceptual, visual processing and visual-motor integration deficits; disorders of attention, concentration and perseverance; delayed emotional development; behavioral disorders; and hyperactivity. Subtle physical, visual and hearing problems can also contribute to early school failure and subsequent behavioral and emotional difficulties.

It is the belief of the SOUTHEASTERN PSYCHOLOGICAL INSTITUTE that early identification followed by careful planning, treatment and remediation can eliminate, or significantly minimize, learning, attention, academic, emotional and behavioral problems at the elementary school level when the problems are milder and more amenable to intervention. It can save the child from facing years of school failure which, in turn, can lead to frustration, loss of self-esteem, acting-out, and other emotional difficulties. Early identification and intervention, likewise, spare families the pain and frustration of feeling they are responsible but helpless to change things. In addition, improvement occurs rapidly at younger ages.

Parents are the first to recognize that something is not "exactly right" with their child. However, they frequently do not know whether their concerns are really significant, which things the child will "grow out of", and which warrant professional consultation.

The Symptom Checklist for Developmental Disabilities was developed by Dr. Edna Copeland, after 15 years of clinical practice, to help parents and teachers determine whether their children or the children they teach have developmental difficulties that are either learning, attentional, behavioral, social or emotional in nature.

If you have checked many items and have concerns after completing this questionnaire, you are encouraged to discuss your child's development with his/her teacher and/or pediatrician, or a child psychologist. Addressing even mild developmental delays early is crucial for the child's ultimate welfare. Determining strengths is, likewise, important.

SYMPTOM CHECKLIST

This checklist was developed from the experience of many specialists in the fields which comprise Developmental Disabilities. The questions asked are warning signals of conditions which may interfere with your child's academic, emotional and social adjustment now and in the future.

If you answer "Yes" to as many as 20% of the questions, it may mean that your child has a Developmental Disability. A Developmental Disability does not mean that a child is lacking in intelligence or capability. Rather, it means that a child may have difficulty achieving academically and socially at his/her level of ability.

Directions: Place a checkmark (✓) by those questions to which your answer is "Yes." Do not mark questions to which you answer "No."

SYMPTOM CHECKLIST FOR DEVELOPMENTAL DISABILITIES

I. ATTENTION/CONCENTRATION/IMPULSE CONTROL/BEHAVIOR

1. Does your child interrupt frequently?
2. Is your child easily distracted?
3. Is your child up and down frequently during meals?
4. Is your child's work often sloppy although it can be neat if he/she really tries?
5. Does your child move from activity to activity without settling down to any one thing for long?
6. Is there inconsistency in your child's performance, i.e., 'one day he/she performs a task well, the next day, he/she performs the same task poorly?
7. Does your child have difficulty playing alone?
8. Was your child not cuddly as an infant?
9. Did your child require little sleep as an infant?
10. Is your child more demanding than other children?
11. Is punishment ineffective with your child?
12. Is your child always better in a one-to-one situation?
13. Does your child "fidget" a lot?
14. Does your child often fail to finish things he/she starts?
15. Does your child have difficulty concentrating on tasks requiring sustained attention?
16. Is your child excitable and impulsive?
17. Is your child immature for his/her age?
18. Does your child's mood change quickly and drastically?
19. Is your child more active than his/her peers?
20. Does your child become frustrated easily?
21. Does your child have poor self-control?
22. Is your child extremely daring?
23. Is your child a discipline problem?
24. Does your child find it necessary to touch everything he/she sees?
25. Does your child bother other children — either by touching them or intruding into their activities and conversations?
26. Does your child have difficulty waiting his turn in games or group situations?
27. Do birthday parties and situations with a lot of stimulation cause your child to become overly excited and lose control?
28. Is your child consistently less active than other children?

II. SOCIAL/EMOTIONAL

1. Is your child rejected or ignored by peers and/or adults?
2. Is your child beginning to think of himself as "mean" or "dumb"?
3. Does your child deny mistakes or blame others?
4. Does your child's mood change quickly and drastically?
5. Does your child have temper tantrums?
6. Does your child show many fears or one unreasonable fear?
7. Does your child bully others?
8. Is your child purposely destructive or hurtful of animals or people?
9. Is your child withdrawn, apathetic, or "off in his own world"?
10. Does your child seem sad or worried much of the time?
11. Does your child have frequent nightmares or other sleep disturbance?
12. Does your child seem irresponsible, undependable, or disorganized?
13. Does your child have a precocious interest in sex or seem to have sexual identity problems?
14. Is your child resistant to discipline or directions; is he/she defiant, resentful or uncooperative?
15. Has your child lost interest in activities with his/her friends and family?

III. HEARING/AUDITORY PERCEPTION/AUDITORY PROCESSING

1. Does your child have trouble remembering things?
2. Does your child seem to "tune-out" or daydream at times?
3. Was your child's speech late or abnormal in any way?
4. Did your child have chronic ear infections during any time from birth to age 6?
5. Was your child late in learning his/her colors, numbers or alphabet?

A CHECK UP for ADOLESCENTS

A SYMPTOM CHECKLIST FOR BEHAVIORAL, ATTENTIONAL, LEARNING AND EMOTIONAL DIFFICULTIES

by

Edna D. Copeland, Ph.D., Director
Child/Clinical Psychologist

Southeastern Psychological Institute
P.O. Box 12389
Atlanta, Georgia 30355-2389
(404) 256-4333

Dedicated to Prevention through Early Intervention™

© Copyright, Edna D. Copeland, Ph.D., 1984, 1987
Published by SPI, P. O. Box 12389, Atlanta, GA 30355-2389

---

7. Do other people have difficulty understanding your teen's speech?

8. Do you often have to repeat directions for your adolescent?

9. Does it seem that your teen pays very little attention to you?

10. Is your teen unable to modulate his/her voice, i.e., speak softly when in quiet situations and louder when needed to be heard?

11. Does your adolescent talk very loudly, even during normal conversations?

12. When called from another room, does your teen frequently not respond?

13. Does your teen frequently turn the same ear in the direction of sound?

14. Does your teen complain that his ears hurt or ring?

15. Is there a history of hearing or auditory processing problems in your family?

IV. VISION/VISUAL PERCEPTION/ VISUAL PROCESSING/VISUAL- MOTOR SKILLS

1. Does your teen have little interest in puzzles, VCR's and other mechanical things?

2. Did your teen have difficulty learning to recognize colors, shapes, letters and numbers?

3. Does your teen confuse letters, numbers, shapes or words which are similar?

4. Are your adolescent's drawings immature and lacking in detail?

5. Does your child have difficulty recognizing letters, numbers, shapes, words or objects if parts are missing?

6. Does/did your teen reverse letters (b/d), numbers (6/9), or words (saw/was)?

7. Did your teen have difficulty learning right and left?

8. Does your adolescent get lost easily or seem confused about directions?

9. Does your teen have a poor concept of time?

10. Are your teen's verbal abilities much better than written expression? Does s/he dislike writing?

11. Does your teen have difficulty writing as well as his peers?

12. Does your teen avoid games or activities involving catching or throwing a ball?

13. Does your adolescent squint when looking at the board or far away objects?

14. Is there a history of visual or visual processing problems in your family?

15. Does your child prefer seeing things to listening to explanations?

V. ACADEMIC ACHIEVEMENT

1. Is your teen's academic achievement below the level you had expected based on ability? Do the teachers say, "S/he is not working up to potential?"

2. Is your teen's daily performance in school inconsistent?

3. Is your adolescent having difficulty reading or understanding what s/he reads?

4. Does your teen seem afraid or embarrassed to ask questions at school?

5. Does your teen follow academic directions poorly?

6. Does your adolescent dislike school?

7. Does your teen have difficulty with math but enjoy reading and spelling?

8. Does your teen have difficulty completing class assignments within the allotted time?

9. Has your adolescent's teacher expressed concern about any area of academic performance?

10. Has your teen had difficulty adjusting to classroom routine and discipline?

VI. MEDICAL

1. Does your teen get frequent headaches and/or stomachaches?

2. Is your adolescent always tired?

3. Was your teen late in establishing bowel and bladder control?

4. Does your teen have a poor appetite?

5. Does your teen have a history of anemia of any type?

6. Is your adolescent irritable before and/or shortly after meals?

7. Does your teen crave sweets?

8. Was your teen an unusually cranky, difficult baby?

9. Was your teen an unusually passive baby, toddler and preschooler?

10. Does your teen have a history of allergies?

11. Is there a history of allergies in the family?

12. Is there a history of diabetes in the family?

Name of Child: _____

Date: _____

Completed by: _____

IDENTIFICATION OF LEARNING, BEHAVIORAL AND EMOTIONAL DISORDERS TO FACILITATE REMEDIATION, TREATMENT AND EDUCATION.

It is becoming increasingly apparent that many problems of adolescence including school failure, behavioral difficulties, delinquency, drug and alcohol abuse, and problems in social and peer relationships have their origins in developmental disabilities of attention and learning. These disorders include learning disabilities; communicative disorders; visual-perceptual/visual processing problems; disorders of attention, concentration, and perseverance; and continued problems of activity level. Subtle and ongoing physical or medical conditions, as well as vision and hearing problems, can also contribute substantially to school failure and behavioral or emotional difficulties.

It is the belief of the that identification of difficulties, followed by careful planning, treatment and remediation can eliminate, or significantly minimize, learning, attention, academic, emotional and behavioral problems. It can save the adolescent from facing even more years of school failure which, in turn, can lead to frustration, loss of self-esteem, acting-out, school dropout and other emotional difficulties. Identification and intervention, likewise, spare families the pain and frustration of feeling they are responsible but helpless to change things. In addition, improvement often occurs rapidly once interventions are begun.

Parents are the first to recognize that something is not "exactly right" with their adolescent. However, they frequently do not know whether their concerns are really significant, which issues are merely part of being an adolescent, and which warrant professional consultation.

A Checklist for Adolescents was developed by Dr. Edna Copeland, after 20 years of clinical practice, to help parents and teachers determine whether their teens or the teens they teach have difficulties that are either learning, attentional, behavioral, social or emotional in both nature and origin.

If you have checked many items and have concerns after completing this questionnaire, you are encouraged to discuss your teen's development with his/her teacher and/or physician, counselor or a psychologist. Addressing even mild concerns early is crucial for the adolescent's ultimate welfare. Determining strengths is, likewise, important.

SYMPTOM CHECKLIST FOR DEVELOPMENTAL DISABILITIES

This checklist was developed from the experience of many specialists in the fields of education, medicine and psychology, among others. The questions asked are warning signals of conditions which may interfere with your teen's academic, emotional, social and life adjustment now and in the future.

If you answer "yes" to as many as 20% of the questions, it may mean that your teen has difficulties which need attention. It does not mean that the adolescent is lacking in intelligence or capability. Rather, it means that s/he may have difficulty achieving academically and socially at his/her level of ability.

Directions: Place a checkmark (✓) by those questions to which your answer is "Yes." Do not mark questions to which you answer "No".

I. ATTENTION/CONCENTRATION/IMPULSE CONTROL/BEHAVIOR

1. Does your teen interrupt frequently?
2. Is your adolescent easily distracted?
3. Is your teen up and down frequently during meals?
4. Is your teen's work often sloppy although it can be neat if s/he really tries?
5. Does your teen move from activity to activity without settling down to any one thing for long?
6. Is there inconsistency in your adolescent's performance, i.e., one day s/he performs a task well, the next day, s/he performs the same task poorly?
7. Does your teen have difficulty being alone?
8. Is your teen aloof and unapproachable?
9. Does your teen require little sleep?
10. Is your teen more demanding than others his/her age?
11. Is punishment ineffective with your adolescent?
12. Is your teen always better in a one-to-one situation?
13. Does your teen "fidget" a lot?
14. Does your teen often fail to finish things s/he starts?
15. Does your teen have difficulty concentrating on tasks requiring sustained attention?
16. Is your adolescent excitable and impulsive?
17. Is your teen immature for his/her age?
18. Is your adolescent sluggish and listless?
19. Is your teen more active than his/her peers?
20. Does your teen become frustrated easily?
21. Does your teen have poor self-control?
22. Is your adolescent extremely daring?
23. Is your teen a discipline problem?
24. Does your teen find it necessary to touch everything s/he sees?
25. Does your teen irritate others — either by touching them or intruding into their activities and conversations?
26. Does your teen still have difficulty waiting his turn in games or group situations?
27. Do parties and other situations with a lot of stimulation cause your teen to become overly excited and lose control?
28. Is your adolescent consistently less active than other children?

II. SOCIAL/EMOTIONAL

1. Is your teen rejected or ignored by peers and/or adults?
2. Is your teen beginning to think of himself as "stupid" or lacking in ability?
3. Does your adolescent deny mistakes or blame others?
4. Does your teen's mood change quickly and drastically?
5. Is your teen easily angered when things don't go his/her way?
6. Does your teen show many fears or one unreasonable fear?
7. Does your adolescent bully others?
8. Is your teen purposely destructive or hurtful of animals or people?
9. Is your teen withdrawn, apathetic, or "off in his own world"?
10. Does your teen seem sad or worried much of the time?
11. Does your teen have frequent nightmares or other sleep disturbances?
12. Does your adolescent seem irresponsible, undependable or disorganized?
13. Does your teen have an unusual interest in sex or seem to have sexual identity problems?
14. Is your teen resistant to discipline or directions; is s/he defiant, resentful or uncooperative?
15. Has your teen lost more interest than most adolescents in activities with his/her friends and family?

III. HEARING/AUDITORY PERCEPTION/AUDITORY PROCESSING

1. Does your teen have trouble remembering things?
2. Does your adolescent seem to "tune-out" or daydream at times?
3. Was your teen's speech late or abnormal in any way?
4. Did your teen have chronic ear infections during any time from birth to age 6?
5. Did your teen have trouble learning phonics?
6. Does your adolescent frequently mishear directions or conversations?

COPELAND SYMPTOM CHECKLIST FOR ATTENTION DEFICIT DISORDERS

Attention Deficit Hyperactivity Disorder (ADHD)
and Undifferentiated Attention Deficit Disorder (ADD)

This checklist was developed from the experience of many specialists in the field of Attention Deficit Disorders and Hyperactivity. It is designed to help you assess whether your child/student has ADHD or ADD, to what degree, and if so, in which area(s) difficulties are experienced. Please mark all statements. Thank you for your assistance in completing this information.

Name of Child_____ **Date**_____

Completed by _____

Directions: Place a checkmark (✓) by each item below, indicating the degree to which the behavior is characteristic of your child/student.

* denotes ADD with Hyperactivity (ADHD).
• denotes ADD without Hyperactivity (Undifferentiated ADD)

	Not at all	Just a little	Pretty much	Very much	Score	%
I. INATTENTION/DISTRACTIBILITY						
*• 1. A short attention span, especially for low-interest activities.						
*• 2. Difficulty completing tasks.						
• 3. Daydreaming.						
*• 4. Easily distracted.						
• 5. Nicknames such as: "spacey," or "dreamer."						
*• 6. Engages in much activity but accomplishes little.						
*• 7. Enthusiastic beginnings but poor endings.					21	%
II. IMPULSIVITY						
* 1. Excitability.						
*• 2. Low frustration tolerance.						
*• 3. Acts before thinking.						
*• 4. Disorganization.						
*• 5. Poor planning ability.						
*• 6. Excessively shifts from one activity to another.						
* 7. Difficulty in group situations which require patience and taking turns.						
*• 8. Requires much supervision.						
*• 9. Constantly in trouble for deeds of omission as well as deeds of commission.						
*• 10. Frequently interrupts conversations; talks out of turn.					30	%
III. ACTIVITY LEVEL PROBLEMS						
A. Overactivity/Hyperactivity						
*• 1. Restlessness — either fidgetiness or being constantly on the go.						
* 2. Diminished need for sleep.						
* 3. Excessive talking.						
* 4. Excessive running, jumping and climbing.						
* 5. Motor restlessness during sleep. Kicks covers off — moves around constantly.						
* 6. Difficulty staying seated at meals, in class, etc. Often walks around classroom.					18	%
B. Underactivity						
• 1. Lethargy.						
• 2. Daydreaming, spaciness.						
• 3. Failure to complete tasks.						
*• 4. Inattention.						
*• 5. Poor leadership ability.						
*• 6. Difficulty in learning and performing.					18	%
IV. NON-COMPLIANCE						
*• 1. Frequently disobeys.						
*• 2. Argumentative.						
* 3. Disregards socially-accepted standards of behavior.						
• 4. "Forgets" unintentionally.						
5. Uses "forgetting" as an excuse (intentional).					15	%

Published by **SPI** Southeastern Psychological Institute, P.O. Box 12389, Atlanta, Georgia 30355-2389

COPELAND SYMPTOM CHECKLIST FOR ATTENTION DEFICIT DISORDERS (Continued)

	Not at all	Just a little	Pretty much	Very much
V. ATTENTION-GETTING BEHAVIOR				
• 1. Frequently needs to be the center of attention.				
• 2. Constantly asks questions or interrupts.				
• 3. Irritates and annoys siblings, peers and adults.				
• 4. Behaves as the "class clown."				
• 5. Uses bad or rude language to attract attention.				
• 6. Engages in other negative behaviors to attract attention.				18 = %
VI. IMMATURITY				
•• 1. Behavior resembles that of a younger child. Responses are typical of children 6 months to 2-plus years younger.				
•• 2. Physical development is delayed.				
•• 3. Prefers younger children and relates better to them.				
•• 4. Emotional reactions are often immature.				12 = %
VII. POOR ACHIEVEMENT/COGNITIVE & VISUAL-MOTOR PROBLEMS				
•• 1. Underachieves relative to ability.				
•• 2. Loses books, assignments, etc.				
•• 3. Auditory memory and auditory processing problems.				
•• 4. Learning disabilities/learning problems.				
•• 5. Incomplete assignments.				
•• 6. Academic work completed too quickly.				
•• 7. Academic work completed too slowly.				
•• 8. "Messy" or "sloppy" written work; poor handwriting.				
•• 9. Poor memory for directions, instructions and rote learning.				27 = %
VIII. EMOTIONAL DIFFICULTIES				
•• 1. Frequent and unpredictable mood swings.				
•• 2. High levels of irritability.				
• 3. Underreactive to pain/insensitive to danger.				
• 4. Easily overstimulated. Hard to calm down once over-excited.				
•• 5. Low frustration tolerance.				
• 6. Temper tantrums, angry outbursts.				
• 7. Moodiness.				
•• 8. Low self-esteem.				24 = %
IX. POOR PEER RELATIONS				
• 1. Hits, bites, or kicks other children.				
• 2. Difficulty following the rules of games and social interactions.				
•• 3. Rejected or avoided by peers.				
• 4. Avoids group activities; a loner.				
• 5. Teases peers and siblings excessively.				
• 6. Bullies or bosses other children.				18 = %
X. FAMILY INTERACTION PROBLEMS				
1. Frequent family conflict.				
2. Activities and social gatherings are unpleasant.				
3. Parents argue over discipline since nothing works.				
4. Mother spends hours and hours on homework with ADD child leaving little time for others in family.				
5. Meals are frequently unpleasant.				
6. Arguments occur between parents and child over responsibilities and chores.				
7. Stress is continuous from child's social and academic problems.				
8. Parents, especially mother, feel: [ ] frustrated [ ] hopeless [ ] alone [ ] angry [ ] guilty [ ] afraid for child [ ] helpless [ ] disappointed [ ] sad and depressed				24 = %

SPI

COPELAND SYMPTOM CHECKLIST
FOR ADULT ATTENTION DEFICIT DISORDERS

Attention Deficit Hyperactivity Disorder (ADHD)
and Undifferentiated Attention Deficit Disorder (ADD)

This checklist was developed from the experience of many specialists in the field of Attention Disorders and Hyperactivity. It is designed to help determine whether you, or someone you are rating, has ADHD or ADD, to what degree, and if so, in which area(s) difficulties are experienced. Please mark all statements. Thank you for your assistance in completing this information.

Name _____ Date _____

Completed by _____

Directions: Place a checkmark (✔) by each item below, indicating the degree to which the behavior is characteristic of yourself or the adult you are rating.

	Not at all	Just a little	Pretty much	Very much	Score	%
I. INATTENTION/DISTRACTIBILITY, especially						
1. A short attention span, especially for low-interest activities.						
2. Difficulty completing tasks.						
3. Daydreaming.						
4. Easily distracted.						
5. Nicknames such as: "spacey," or "dreamer."						
6. Engages in much activity but accomplishes little.						
7. Enthusiastic beginnings but poor endings.					21 = %
II. IMPULSIVITY						
1. Excitability.						
2. Low frustration tolerance.						
3. Acts before thinking.						
4. Disorganization.						
5. Poor planning ability.						
6. Excessively shifts from one activity to another.						
7. Difficulty in group situations which require patience and taking turns.						
8. Interrupts frequently.					24 = %
III. ACTIVITY LEVEL PROBLEMS						
A. Overactivity/Hyperactivity						
1. Restlessness — either fidgetiness or being constantly on the go.						
2. Diminished need for sleep.						
3. Excessive talking.						
4. Difficulty listening.						
5. Motor restlessness during sleep. Kicks covers off — moves around constantly.						
6. Dislike of situations which require attention & being still—church, lectures, etc.					18 = %
B. Underactivity						
1. Lethargic.						
2. Daydreaming, spaciness.						
3. Failure to complete tasks.						
4. Inattention.						
5. Lacking in leadership.						
6. Difficulty in getting things done.					18 = %

Copyright ©1989 by Edna D. Copeland, Ph.D.

Published by **SPI** Southeastern Psychological Institute, P.O. Box 12389, Atlanta, Georgia 30355-2389

COPELAND SYMPTOM CHECKLIST FOR ADULT ATTENTION DEFICIT DISORDERS (Continued)

	Not at all	Just a little	Pretty much	Very much
IV. NONCOMPLIANCE				
1. Does not cooperate. Determined to do things own way.				
2. Argumentative.				
3. Disregards socially-accepted behavioral expectations.				
4. "Forgets" unintentionally.				
5. "Forgets" as an excuse (intentionally).				

_____ = ____%
10

	Not at all	Just a little	Pretty much	Very much
V. UNDERACHIEVEMENT/DISORGANIZATION/LEARNING PROBLEMS				
1. Underachievement in relation to ability.				
2. Frequent job changes.				
3. Loses things — keys, wallet, lists, belongings, etc.				
4. Auditory memory and auditory processing problems.				
5. Learning disabilities or learning problems.				
6. Poor handwriting.				
7. "Messy" or "sloppy" work.				
8. Work assignments are often not completed satisfactorily.				
9. Rushes through work.				
10. Works too slowly.				
11. Procrastinates. Bills, taxes, etc., put off until the last minute.				

_____ = ____%
33

	Not at all	Just a little	Pretty much	Very much
VI. EMOTIONAL DIFFICULTIES				
1. Frequent and unpredictable mood swings.				
2. Irritability.				
3. Underreactive to pain/insensitive to danger.				
4. Easily overstimulated. Hard to stop once "revved up."				
5. Low frustration tolerance. Excessive emotional reaction to frustrating situations.				
6. Angry outbursts.				
7. Moodiness/lack of energy.				
8. Low self-esteem.				
9. Immaturity.				

_____ = ____%
27

	Not at all	Just a little	Pretty much	Very much
VII. POOR PEER RELATIONS				
1. Difficulty following the rules of social interactions.				
2. Rejected or avoided by peers.				
3. Avoids group activities; a loner.				
4. "Bosses" other people. Wants to be the leader.				
5. Critical of others.				

_____ = ____%
15

	Not at all	Just a little	Pretty much	Very much
VIII. IMPAIRED FAMILY RELATIONSHIPS				
1. Easily frustrated with spouse or children. Overreacts. May punish children too severely.				
2. Sees things from own point of view. Does not negotiate differences well.				
3. Underdeveloped sense of responsibility.				
4. Poor manager of money.				
5. Unreasonable; demanding.				
6. Spends excessive amount of time at work because of inefficiency, leaving little time for family.				

_____ = ____%
18

 Published by **SPI** Southeastern Psychological Institute, P.O. Box 12389, Atlanta, Georgia 30355-2389

SPI

SCORING THE COPELAND SYMPTOM CHECKLIST FOR ATTENTION DEFICIT DISORDERS (ADHD/ADD)
(Child/Adolescent Checklist and Adult Checklist)

1. Scores for each category are as follows:

   Not at all = 0;   Just a little = 1;   Pretty much = 2;   Very much = 3

2. Each check receives a score from 0 - 3. Add the checks in each category. That score is placed over the total possible. Example:

	0 Not at all	1 Just a little	2 Pretty much	3 Very much	Score	%
* denotes ADD with Hyperactivity (ADHD). • denotes ADD without Hyperactivity (Undifferentiated ADD)						
I. INATTENTION/DISTRACTIBILITY						
*• 1. A short attention span, especially for low-interest activities.				✓		
*• 2. Difficulty completing tasks.			✓			
• 3. Daydreaming.		✓				
*• 4. Easily distracted.				✓		
• 5. Nicknames such as: "spacey," or "dreamer."		✓				
*• 6. Engages in much activity but accomplishes little.				✓		
*• 7. Enthusiastic beginnings but poor endings.				✓	16 / 21	76 %
II. IMPULSIVITY						
* 1. Excitability.				✓		
*• 2. Low frustration tolerance.				✓		
*• 3. Acts before thinking.				✓		
*• 4. Disorganization.			✓			
*• 5. Poor planning ability.			✓			
*• 6. Excessively shifts from one activity to another.				✓		
* 7. Difficulty in group situations which require patience and taking turns.				✓		
*• 8. Requires much supervision.				✓		
*• 9. Constantly in trouble for deeds of omission as well as deeds of commission.			✓			
*•10. Frequently interrupts conversations; talks out of turn.				✓	27 / 30	90 %

3. Compute the percentage for each category.

   Significance:*

   Scores between 35-49% suggest mild to moderate difficulties.

   Scores between 50-69% suggest moderate to severe difficulties.

   Scores above 70% suggest major interference.

   (*These scores represent clinical significance. The scale is currently being normed and statistical data should be available soon.)

   Children, adolescents and adults may have difficulties in only one area or in all ten. Those with undifferentiated ADD on the more daydreaming, inattentive, anxious end of the ADD continuum frequently manifest difficulties only in the "Inattention/Distractibility", "Underactivity", and the "Underachievement" categories, while those with overactive, impulsive ADHD will have difficulties in many more areas of their lives.

Published by SPI Southeastern Psychological Institute, P.O. Box 12389, Atlanta, Georgia 30355-2389

MEDICATION

Child's Name: _____

MEDICATION SCHEDULE

Instructions Re: Medicine

Month: _____ Year: _____

Parents and Teachers

Please complete Abbreviated Parent and Behavior
Rating Scales every day, including those days when
no medicine is taken.

SUNDAY	MONDAY	TUESDAY	WEDNESDAY	THURSDAY	FRIDAY	SATURDAY

Copeland Medication Follow-Up Questionnaire
Teacher/Parent
Weekly Record Form

Copyright © 1991 by Edna D. Copeland, Ph.D.

Child's Name _____

Date _____ to _____
month/day   month/day

Completed by _____ Date _____
month/day

Please indicate E — excellent; G — good; F — fair; P — poor

Day	Medication Schedule (specify (1) Name of medication; (2) Dose; and (3) Time medication is to be taken)	Attention/Ability to Focus	Impulse Control	Activity Level (Over/Under)	Compliance/Cooperation	Organization	Peer/Sibling Relations	Completing and Turning in School Work	Grades (Weekly or periodic comments to be written out)
Mon. a.m.									
p.m.									
Tues. a.m.									
p.m.									
Wed. a.m.									
p.m.									
Thurs. a.m.									
p.m.									
Fri. a.m.									
p.m.									
Sat. a.m.									
p.m.									
Sun. a.m.									
p.m.									Please put any additional comments on the back of this sheet.

ATTENTION DISORDERS (ADHD/ADD) MEDICATION SIDE EFFECTS

Child/Adolescent's Name_____ Date_____

Medication _____

☐ Tablet ☐ Time-Release_____ Dose: A.M._____mg. P.M._____mg. Evening_____mg.

Completed by: (Name)_____ (Position)_____

SIDE EFFECTS

When medication is used, side effects sometimes occur. If any of the side effects listed below is observed, please indicate which one(s) occurred and the severity of it. If any other side effect occurs, please write it in the space provided.

	Not at all	Just a little	Pretty much	Very much	Don't Know
A. Decreased appetite					
Weight loss					
Insomnia (inability to fall asleep)					
Fitful sleeping					
Difficulty awakening					
Nightmares					
B. Headaches					
Stomachaches					
Tics or involuntary motor movements, e.g., eyeblink					
Dizziness					
Rashes					
Bedwetting					
C. Irritability					
Feeling anxious, "jittery"					
Restlessness					
Tenseness					
Heart racing					
Socially withdrawn					
Sadness					
Other					

Published by **SPI** Southeastern Psychological Institute, P.O. Box 12389, Atlanta, Georgia 30305-2389

RESPONSIBILITY PROGRAMS

_____   _____
(Name)   (Week of)

My Responsibilities

Morning:	Mon.	Tues.	Wed.	Thu.	Fri.	Sat.	Sun.
1. Get up by _____ with alarm clock.	____	____	____	____	____	____	____
2. Get dressed and to breakfast by _____.	____	____	____	____	____	____	____
3. Grooming							
a. Wash face	____	____	____	____	____	____	____
b. Brush teeth	____	____	____	____	____	____	____
c. Comb hair	____	____	____	____	____	____	____
d. _____	____	____	____	____	____	____	____
4. Put pajamas away (dirty clothes in hamper, etc.).	____	____	____	____	____	____	____
5. Make bed.	____	____	____	____	____	____	____
6. Straighten room. (A = 3✓'s; B = 2✓'s; C = 1✓)	____	____	____	____	____	____	____
7. Empty trash can on _____.	____	____	____	____	____	____	____
8. Use manners at breakfast.	____	____	____	____	____	____	____
9. Remove dishes from table.	____	____	____	____	____	____	____
10. _____	____	____	____	____	____	____	____
11. _____	____	____	____	____	____	____	____
12. _____	____	____	____	____	____	____	____

After School:							
1. Put away books.	____	____	____	____	____	____	____
2. Hang up coat; put clothes away.	____	____	____	____	____	____	____
3. Practice _____ 30 minutes. (3✓'s)	____	____	____	____	____	____	____
4. Do homework (in room). (3✓'s)	____	____	____	____	____	____	____
5. Pick up den and/or playroom daily by _____ P.M.	____	____	____	____	____	____	____
6. Put outside toys away by _____ P.M.	____	____	____	____	____	____	____
7. _____	____	____	____	____	____	____	____
8. _____	____	____	____	____	____	____	____
9. _____	____	____	____	____	____	____	____

Dinner and Bedtime:							
1. Set table for dinner.	____	____	____	____	____	____	____
2. Manners at dinner.	____	____	____	____	____	____	____
3. Remove dishes from table; help clean up kitchen.	____	____	____	____	____	____	____
4. Bath. Dirty clothes in hamper. Clean out tub. (3✓'s)	____	____	____	____	____	____	____
5. Select clothes for next day.	____	____	____	____	____	____	____
6. Get all school papers signed. Put everything together for the next day.	____	____	____	____	____	____	____
7. In bed by _____ or earlier to read.	____	____	____	____	____	____	____
8. Read 15 minutes in book.	____	____	____	____	____	____	____
9. _____	____	____	____	____	____	____	____
10. _____	____	____	____	____	____	____	____
11. _____	____	____	____	____	____	____	____

Behavior and Attitude:							
1. Do what parents request pleasantly.	____	____	____	____	____	____	____
2. Be nice to siblings.	____	____	____	____	____	____	____
3. Don't argue or talk back.	____	____	____	____	____	____	____
4. _____	____	____	____	____	____	____	____
5. _____	____	____	____	____	____	____	____
6. _____	____	____	____	____	____	____	____

Extra Responsibilities/Weekend:							
1. _____	____	____	____	____	____	____	____
2. _____	____	____	____	____	____	____	____
3. _____	____	____	____	____	____	____	____
4. _____	____	____	____	____	____	____	____
5. _____	____	____	____	____	____	____	____
6. _____	____	____	____	____	____	____	____

VALUES: 6✓'s = _____
MY DAILY TOTAL | | | | | | | |

RESPONSIBILITIES HELP YOU BECOME THE BEST YOU CAN BE . . .

Confident, Capable, Cooperative

FOR INFORMATION OR REPRODUCTION OF ANY PART OF THIS MATERIAL, CONTACT
3 C's OF CHILDHOOD INC., P.O. BOX 12389, ATLANTA, GEORGIA 30355-2389

_____   _____
(Name)   (Week of)

Teen Responsibilities

MORNING:	Mon.	Tues.	Wed.	Thur.	Fri.	Sat.	Sun.
1. Get up early enough to complete jobs.	____	____	____	____	____	____	____
2. Grooming:							
a. Wash face	____	____	____	____	____	____	____
b. Brush teeth	____	____	____	____	____	____	____
c. Wash/dry hair	____	____	____	____	____	____	____
d. _____	____	____	____	____	____	____	____
3. Make bed.	____	____	____	____	____	____	____
4. Straighten room.	____	____	____	____	____	____	____
5. Straighten bathroom.	____	____	____	____	____	____	____
6. Get dressed and to breakfast by _____ A.M.	____	____	____	____	____	____	____
7. Eat healthy breakfast.	____	____	____	____	____	____	____
8. Remove dishes/clean kitchen.	____	____	____	____	____	____	____
9. Take vitamins/medicine.	____	____	____	____	____	____	____
10. _____	____	____	____	____	____	____	____
11. _____	____	____	____	____	____	____	____
12. _____	____	____	____	____	____	____	____

AFTER SCHOOL/DINNER/EVENING							
1. Put books away.	____	____	____	____	____	____	____
2. Hang up coat; put clothes, sports equipment, etc. away.	____	____	____	____	____	____	____
3. Do homework.	____	____	____	____	____	____	____
4. Set table by _____ P.M. for dinner.	____	____	____	____	____	____	____
5. Manners at dinner.	____	____	____	____	____	____	____
6. Remove dishes from table. Clean or help clean kitchen.	____	____	____	____	____	____	____
7. Get all papers signed; review next day with parents.	____	____	____	____	____	____	____
8. Get organized and ready for next day; books in chair; clothes for activities, etc.	____	____	____	____	____	____	____
9. In bed by _____ P.M.	____	____	____	____	____	____	____
10. _____	____	____	____	____	____	____	____
11. _____	____	____	____	____	____	____	____
12. _____	____	____	____	____	____	____	____

WEEKLY/WEEKEND							
1. Cook dinner on _____.	____	____	____	____	____	____	____
2. Cook breakfast on _____.	____	____	____	____	____	____	____
3. Keep weekly budget of income and expenses.	____	____	____	____	____	____	____
4. Plan calendar and "To Do" list for next two weeks.	____	____	____	____	____	____	____
5. Participate in meal planning.	____	____	____	____	____	____	____
6. Thank you calls/notes:							
_____	____	____	____	____	____	____	____
_____	____	____	____	____	____	____	____
_____	____	____	____	____	____	____	____
7. Clean own bedroom and bath: change sheets, vacuum, dust, straighten closets and drawers; clean bathroom.	____	____	____	____	____	____	____
8. Garbage can to street on _____.	____	____	____	____	____	____	____
9. Garbage can from street on _____.	____	____	____	____	____	____	____
10. Brush/bathe pet.	____	____	____	____	____	____	____
11. Collect, sort and wash dirty clothes.	____	____	____	____	____	____	____
12. Take clothes from dryer, sort, fold and put away.	____	____	____	____	____	____	____
13. Iron.	____	____	____	____	____	____	____
14. _____	____	____	____	____	____	____	____
15. _____	____	____	____	____	____	____	____
16. _____	____	____	____	____	____	____	____

BEHAVIOR/ATTITUDE/MANNERS							
1. Greet parents with handshake or hug.	____	____	____	____	____	____	____
2. Do what is requested pleasantly.	____	____	____	____	____	____	____
3. Be nice to siblings.	____	____	____	____	____	____	____
4. Music at _____ decibels.	____	____	____	____	____	____	____
5. Answer telephone appropriately. Be pleasant and courteous to callers.	____	____	____	____	____	____	____
6. Leave messages.	____	____	____	____	____	____	____
7. Come in on time (Curfew: _____)	____	____	____	____	____	____	____
8. _____	____	____	____	____	____	____	____
9. _____	____	____	____	____	____	____	____

VALUES: 6 ✓'s = _____

DAILY TOTAL							

SUCCESS IN ADULTHOOD IS DIRECTLY RELATED TO THE AMOUNT OF
MEANINGFUL WORK DONE IN CHILDHOOD AND ADOLESCENCE.

—Harvard Report

SUPPLEMENT TO THE AUDIOPROGRAM "THE JOY OF A JOB WELL DONE: TEACHING YOUR CHILD THE
VALUE OF WORK AND RESPONSIBILITY" AND BEHAVIOR INCENTIVE PROGRAM
FOR INFORMATION OR REPRODUCTION OF ANY PART OF THIS MATERIAL, PLEASE CONTACT 3C's OF CHILDHOOD, INC.
P.O. BOX 12389, ATLANTA, GA. 30355-2389 (404) 256-0903

Family Organization Calendar

GETTING OUR FAMILY ORGANIZED

(MONTH) _____ (YEAR) _____

	MONDAY	TUESDAY	WEDNESDAY	THURSDAY	FRIDAY	SATURDAY	SUNDAY
WEEK 1:	ACTIVITIES: / TO DO:	ACTIVITIES: / TO DO:	ACTIVITIES: / TO DO:	ACTIVITIES: / TO DO:	ACTIVITIES: / TO DO:	ACTIVITIES: / TO DO:	ACTIVITIES: / TO DO:
WEEK 2:	ACTIVITIES: / TO DO:	ACTIVITIES: / TO DO:	ACTIVITIES: / TO DO:	ACTIVITIES: / TO DO:	ACTIVITIES: / TO DO:	ACTIVITIES: / TO DO:	ACTIVITIES: / TO DO:
WEEK 3:	ACTIVITIES: / TO DO:	ACTIVITIES: / TO DO:	ACTIVITIES: / TO DO:	ACTIVITIES: / TO DO:	ACTIVITIES: / TO DO:	ACTIVITIES: / TO DO:	ACTIVITIES: / TO DO:
WEEK 4:	ACTIVITIES: / TO DO:	ACTIVITIES: / TO DO:	ACTIVITIES: / TO DO:	ACTIVITIES: / TO DO:	ACTIVITIES: / TO DO:	ACTIVITIES: / TO DO:	ACTIVITIES: / TO DO:
WEEK 5:	ACTIVITIES: / TO DO:	ACTIVITIES: / TO DO:	ACTIVITIES: / TO DO:	ACTIVITIES: / TO DO:	ACTIVITIES: / TO DO:	ACTIVITIES: / TO DO:	ACTIVITIES: / TO DO:

TO DO

WEEK 1: _____

WEEK 2: _____

WEEK 3: _____

TO DO:

WEEK 3 (Continued): _____

WEEK 4: _____

WEEK 5: _____

ORGANIZATION HELPS FAMILIES BECOME . . .

CAPABLE
COOPERATIVE
EFFICIENT
And Have More
Time For Fun!

COLOR CODE:

Yellow = _____
Blue = _____
Pink = _____
Green = _____
Orange = _____
Purple = _____

TO GET ORGANIZED:

1. As an activity arises, write it on the calendar.
2. As things occur which need to be done, write them down under "TO DO" on the side. When it is decided when to do them, transfer them to the calendar.
3. Have a "Family Meeting" once a week (Sunday night is best!) to discuss the coming weeks and to get everything scheduled.
4. Choose and/or assign tasks. Color code as assigned.
5. As tasks are completed, cross through with a fine line marker.
6. Group as many tasks as possible to increase efficiency. For example, all gifts and cards for the month can be purchased at the same time. Many errands can be accomplished in one trip.

CLASSROOM MANAGEMENT AND ORGANIZATION

.

EXAMPLE

TODAY'S SCHEDULE

Check As Completed		TO DO	TIME
__ 8:00	Arrive	__ 1. _____	_____
__ 8:15-8:30	Home Room	__ 2. _____	_____
__ 8:30-9:15	Reading Groups	__ 3. _____	_____
__ 9:15-9:20	Break	__ 4. _____	_____
__ 9:20-9:40	Math Plan	__ 5. _____	_____
__ 9:40-10:00	Math Assignment	__ 6. _____	_____
__ 10:00-10:30	Art	__ 7. _____	_____
__ 10:30-11:00	Language Arts	__ 8. _____	_____
__ 11:00-11:30	Wordly Wise Assignments	__ 9. _____	_____
__ 11:30-12:00	Lunch	__ 10. _____	_____
__ 12:00-12:30	Science	__ 11. _____	_____
__ 12:30-1:00	P.E.	__ 12. _____	_____
__ 1:00-1:30	Social Studies	__ 13. _____	_____
__ 1:30-2:00	Music	__ 14. _____	_____
__ 2:00-2:30	Study Period	__ 15. _____	_____
__ 2:30-2:45	Organize for Homework and School Tomorrow	__ 16. _____	_____
__ 2:45	School Over	__ 17. _____	_____

ASSIGNMENTS FOR _____**DATE**_____

MORNING

Work To Do	Order To Do	Time Started	Time Finished	Teacher ✓ Off

AFTER LUNCH

HOMEWORK ASSIGNMENTS

Name:_____

Week of:_____ To:_____
(Month) (Day)   (Month) (Day)

Subjects:	MONDAY	TUESDAY	WEDNESDAY	THURSDAY	FRIDAY
1) Reading					
2) Language					
3) Spelling					
4) Math					
5) Social Studies					
6) Other					
Teacher Initials					
Teacher Comments					
Parent's Initials					

LONG-TERM ASSIGNMENTS:

Due:_____ Assignment:_____

Due:_____ Assignment:_____

TESTS:

Date:_____ Subject:_____   Date:_____ Subject:_____

Date:_____ Subject:_____   Date:_____ Subject:_____

	MONDAY	TUESDAY	WEDNESDAY	THURSDAY	FRIDAY
TAKE TO SCHOOL:					
TAKE HOME:					

Published by SPI Southeastern Psychological Institute, P.O. Box 12389, Atlanta, Georgia 30355-2389

MIDDLE AND HIGH SCHOOL
HOMEWORK ASSIGNMENTS

Name:_____

Week of:_____ To:_____
(Month)   (Day)   (Month)   (Day)

Subjects:	MONDAY	TUESDAY	WEDNESDAY	THURSDAY	FRIDAY
1) _____					
2) _____					
3) _____					
4) _____					
5) _____					
6) _____					

LONG-TERM ASSIGNMENTS:

Due:_____ Assignment:_____

Due:_____ Assignment:_____

TESTS:

Date:_____Subject:_____   Date:_____Subject:_____

Date:_____Subject:_____   Date:_____Subject:_____

	MONDAY	TUESDAY	WEDNESDAY	THURSDAY	FRIDAY
TAKE TO SCHOOL:	_____	_____	_____	_____	_____
	_____	_____	_____	_____	_____
TAKE HOME:	_____	_____	_____	_____	_____
	_____	_____	_____	_____	_____

Published by SPI Southeastern Psychological Institute. P.O. Box 12389, Atlanta, Georgia 30355-2389

NAME: _____   DATE:_____

DAILY HOMEWORK

MATH	SPELLING
SCIENCE	SOCIAL STUDIES
READING	ENGLISH

NAME_____   DATE_____

DAILY

MATH

   Classwork   ___%

   Homework   ___%

   Test/Quiz Grade   ___%

   Comment:_____

   _____

SPELLING

   Classwork   ___%

   Homework   ___%

   Test/Quiz Grade   ___%

   Comment:_____

   _____

SCIENCE

   Classwork   ___%

   Homework   ___%

   Test/Quiz Grade   ___%

   Comment:_____

   _____

SOCIAL STUDIES

   Classwork   ___%

   Homework   ___%

   Test/Quiz Grade   ___%

   Comment:_____

   _____

READING

   Classwork   %

   Homework   ___%

   Test/Quiz Grade   ___%

   Comment:_____

   _____

ENGLISH

   Classwork   ___%

   Homework   ___%

   Test/Quiz Grade   ___%

   Comment:_____

   _____

MATH GRIDS

Name: _____   Date: _____

MATH GRIDS

Name: _____ Date: _____

MATH GRIDS

Name: _____   Date: _____

MATH GRIDS

Name: _____   Date: _____

(Example for Older Children - School)

Daily Progress Report

Name: _____

Week of:_____

Rating Scale:

1 - Excellent   2 - Satisfactory   3 - Unsatisfactory

	Mon.	Tues.	Wed.	Thur.	Fri.
A. Behavior					
1. I was cooperative with the teacher and did *not* argue	—	—	—	—	—
2. I used very good language - no cursing	—	—	—	—	—
3. I was nice to other children - *even* if they were not sometimes	—	—	—	—	—
4. I did what the teacher asked the first time asked	—	—	—	—	—
B. Completed Class Assignments					
1. On time	—	—	—	—	—
2. Neatly	—	—	—	—	—

Positive Consequences:

For 1's ("Excellent"):   2 chips toward an activity or purchase of something special.

For 2's ("Satisfactory"):   1 chip

Negative Consequences:

(1)   If sheet not brought home, in room rest of day with books, toys, radio only.

(2)   "3" - Write 10 times (ex.) "I will try very hard to be cooperative and not argue." 2nd time for same problem write 20 times; 3rd time - write 30 times, etc.

Daily Progress Report

Name: _____

Week of: _____

Rating Scale:

1 - Excellent	2 - Satisfactory	3 - Unsatisfactory

	Mon.	Tues.	Wed.	Thur.	Fri.
A. Behavior					
1.					
2.	—	—	—	—	—
	—	—	—	—	—
3.	—	—	—	—	—
4.	—	—	—	—	—
B. Completed Class Assignments					
1. On time	—	—	—	—	—
2. Neatly	—	—	—	—	—

Positive Consequences:

For 1's (Excellent"):   2 chips toward an activity or purchase of something special.

For 2's ("Satisfactory"):   1 chip

Negative Consequences:

(1) If sheet not brought home, in room rest of day with books, toys, radio only.

(2) 3" - Write 10 times (ex.) "I will try very hard to be cooperative and not argue." 2nd time for same problem write 20 times; 3rd time - write 30 times, etc.

(Example for Younger Children - School)

Daily Progress Report

Name:_____

Week of: _____

Code:

GOOD	OK	POOR

1. I was a good listener.

2. I completed my work on time.

3. I worked without disturbing others.

4. I controlled my talking.

5. I walked in line without pushing and shoving.

I need help in: _____

_____

_____

_____

_____

(Parent's Signature)

Daily Progress Report

Name:_____

Week of: _____

Code:

GOOD   OK   POOR

1.

2.

3.

4.

5.

I need help in: _____

_____

_____

_____

_____
(Parent's Signature)

RESOURCE MATERIAL

National Parent Support Group Associations

Attention Deficit Disorders Association (ADDA)
P. O. Box 488
West Newbury, MA 01985   (800) 487-2282

Children with Attention Deficit Disorders
(CHADD)
499 N.W. 70th Avenue, Suite 308
Plantation, FL 33317   (305) 587-3700

Learning Disabilities Association of
America (LDA)
4156 Library Road
Pittsburgh, PA 15234   (412) 341-1515

Tourette Syndrome Association (TSA)
42-40 Bell Boulevard
Bayside, NY 11361   (718) 224-2999

UNITED STATES DEPARTMENT OF EDUCATION

OFFICE OF SPECIAL EDUCATION AND REHABILITATIVE SERVICES

THE ASSISTANT SECRETARY

MEMORANDUM

SEP 1 6 1991

DATE   :

TO   :   Chief State School Officers

FROM   :   Robert R. Davila
            Assistant Secretary
            Office of Special Education
              and Rehabilitative Services

            Michael L. Williams
            Assistant Secretary
            Office for Civil Rights

            John T. MacDonald
            Assistant Secretary
            Office of Elementary
              and Secondary Education

SUBJECT: Clarification of Policy to Address the Needs of Children with Attention Deficit Disorders
            within General and/or Special Education

I. INTRODUCTION

There is a growing awareness in the education community that attention deficit disorder (ADD) and
attention deficit hyperactive disorder (ADHD) can result in significant learning problems for children
with those conditions.[1] While estimates of the prevalence of ADD vary widely, we believe that three
to five percent of school-aged children may have significant educational problems related to this
disorder. Because ADD has broad implications for education as a whole, the Department believes it
should clarify State and local responsibility under Federal law for addressing the needs of children with
ADD in the schools. Ensuring that these students are able to reach their fullest potential is an inherent
part of the National education goals and AMERICA 2000. The National goals, and the strategy for
achieving them, are based on the assumptions that: (1) all children can learn and benefit from their
education; and (2) the educational community must work to improve the learning opportunities for all
children.

This memorandum clarifies the circumstances under which children with ADD are eligible for special
education services under Part B of the Individuals with Disabilities Education Act (Part B), as well as
the Part B requirements for evaluation of such children's unique educational needs. This memorandum
will also clarify the responsibility of State and local educational agencies (SEAs and LEAs) to provide
special education and related services to eligible children with ADD under Part B. Finally, this
memorandum clarifies the responsibilities of LEAs to provide regular or special education and related
aids and services to those children with ADD who are not eligible under Part B, but who fall within

---

[1]While we recognize that the disorders ADD and ADHD vary, the term ADD is being used to encompass children with both
disorders.

the definition of "handicapped person" under Section 504 of the Rehabilitation Act of 1973. Because of the overall educational responsibility to provide services for these children, it is important that general and special education coordinate their efforts.

II. ELIGIBILITY FOR SPECIAL EDUCATION AND RELATED SERVICES UNDER PART B

Last year during the reauthorization of the Education of the Handicapped Act (now the Individuals with Disabilities Education Act), Congress gave serious consideration to including ADD in the definition of "children with disabilities" in the statute. The Department took the position that ADD does not need to be added as a separate disability category in the statutory definition since children with ADD who require special education and related services can meet the eligibility criteria for services under Part B. This continues to be the Department's position.

No change with respect to ADD was made by Congress in the statutory definition of "children with disabilities;" however, language was included in Section 102(a) of the Education of the Handicapped Act Amendments of 1990 that required the Secretary to issue a Notice of Inquiry (NOI) soliciting public comment on special education for children with ADD under Part B. In response to the NOI (published November 29, 1990 in the *Federal Register*), the Department received over 2000 written comments, which have been transmitted to the Congress. Our review of these written comments indicates that there is confusion in the field regarding the extent to which children with ADD may be served in special education programs conducted under Part B.

A. Description of Part B

Part B requires SEAs and LEAs to make a free appropriate public education (FAPE) available to all eligible children with disabilities and to ensure that the rights and protections of Part B are extended to those children and their parents. 20 U.S.C. 1412(2); 34 CFR §§ 300.121 and 300.2. Under Part B, FAPE, among other elements, includes the provision of special education and related services, at no cost to parents, in conformity with an individualized education program (IEP). 34 CFR § 300.4.

In order to be eligible under Part B, a child must be evaluated in accordance with 34 CFR §§ 300.530-300.534 as having one or more specified physical or mental impairments, and must be found to require special education and related services by reason of one or more of these impairments.[2] 20 U.S.C. 1401(a)(1); 34 CFR § 300.5. SEAs and LEAs must ensure that children with ADD who are determined eligible for services under Part B receive special education and related services designed to meet their unique needs, including special education and related services needs arising from the ADD. A full continuum of placement alternatives, including the regular classroom, must be available for providing special education and related services required in the IEP.

B. Eligibility for Part B services under the "Other Health Impaired" Category

The list of chronic or acute health problems included within the definition of "other health impaired" in the Part B regulations is not exhaustive. The term "other health impaired" includes chronic or acute impairments that result in limited alertness, which adversely affects educational performance. Thus, children with ADD should be classified as eligible for services under the "other health impaired" category in instances where the ADD is a chronic or acute health problem that results in limited alertness, which adversely affects educational performance. In other words, children with ADD, where

---

[2] The Part B regulations define 11 specified disabilities. 34 CFR § 300.5(b)(1)-(11). The Education of the Handicapped Act Amendments of 1990 amended the Individuals with Disabilities Education Act (formerly the Education of the Handicapped Act) to specify that autism and traumatic brain injury are separate disability categories. See section 602(a)(1) of the Act, to be codified at 20 U.S.C. 1401(a)(1).

the ADD is a chronic or acute health problem resulting in limited alertness, may be considered disabled under Part B solely on the basis of this disorder within the "other health impaired" category in situations where special education and related services are needed because of the ADD.

C. Eligibility for Part B services under Other Disability Categories

Children with ADD are also eligible for services under Part B if the children satisfy the criteria applicable to other disability categories. For example, children with ADD are also eligible for services under the "specific learning disability" category of Part B if they meet the criteria stated in §§ 300.5(b)(9) and 300.541 or under the "seriously emotionally disturbed" category of Part B if they meet the criteria stated in § 300.5(b)(8).

III. EVALUATIONS UNDER PART B

A. Requirements

SEAs and LEAs have an affirmative obligation to evaluate a child who is suspected of having a disability to determine the child's need for special education and related services. Under Part B, SEAs and LEAs are required to have procedures for locating, identifying and evaluating all children who have a disability or are suspected of having a disability and are in need of special education and related services. 34 CFR §§ 300.128 and 300.220. This responsibility, known as "child find," is applicable to all children from birth through 21, regardless of the severity of their disability.

Consistent with this responsibility and the obligation to make FAPE available to all eligible children with disabilities, SEAs and LEAs must ensure that evaluations of children who are suspected of needing special education and related services are conducted without undue delay. 20 U.S.C. 1412(2). Because of its responsibility resulting from the FAPE and child find requirements of Part B, a LEA may not refuse to evaluate the possible need for special education and related services of a child with a prior medical diagnosis of ADD solely by reason of that medical diagnosis. However, a medical diagnosis of ADD alone is not sufficient to render a child eligible for services under Part B.

Under Part B, before any action is taken with respect to the initial placement of a child with a disability in a program providing special education and related services, "a full and individual evaluation of the child's educational needs must be conducted in accordance with requirements of § 300.532." 34 CFR § 300.531. Section 300.532(a) requires that a child's evaluation must be conducted by a multidisciplinary team, including at least one teacher or other specialist with knowledge in the area of suspected disability.

B. Disagreements over Evaluations

Any proposal or refusal of any agency to initiate or change the identification, evaluation, or educational placement of the child, or the provision of FAPE to the child is subject to the written prior notice requirements of 34 CFR §§ 300.504-300.505.[3] If a parent disagrees with the LEA's refusal to evaluate a child or the LEA's evaluation and determination that a child does not have a disability for which the

---

[3] Section 300.505 of the Part B regulations sets out the elements that must be contained in the prior written notice to parents:

(1) A full explanation of all of the procedural safeguards available to the parents under Subpart E;
(2) A description of the action proposed or refused by the agency, an explanation of why the agency proposes or refuses to take the action, and a description of any options the agency considered and the reasons why those options were rejected;
(3) A description of each evaluation procedure, test, record, or report the agency uses as a basis for the proposal or refusal; and
(4) A description of any other factors which are relevant to the agency's proposal or refusal.

34 CFR § 300.505(a)(1)-(4).

child is eligible for services under Part B, the parent may request a due process hearing pursuant to 34 CFR §§ 300.506-300.513 of the Part B regulations.

IV. OBLIGATIONS UNDER SECTION 504 OF SEAS AND LEAS TO CHILDREN WITH ADD FOUND NOT TO REQUIRE SPECIAL EDUCATION AND RELATED SERVICES UNDER PART B

Even if a child with ADD is found not to be eligible for services under Part B, the requirements of Section 504 of the Rehabilitation Act of 1973 (Section 504) and its implementing regulation at 34 CFR Part 104 may be applicable. Section 504 prohibits discrimination on the basis of handicap by recipients of Federal funds. Since Section 504 is a civil rights law, rather than a funding law, its requirements are framed in different terms than those of Part B. While the Section 504 regulation was written with an eye to consistency with Part B, it is more general, and there are some differences arising from the differing natures of the two laws. For instance, the protections of Section 504 extend to some children who do not fall within the disability categories specified in Part B.

A. **Definition**

Section 504 requires every recipient that operates a public elementary or secondary education program to address the needs of children who are considered "handicapped persons" under Section 504 as adequately as the needs of nonhandicapped persons are met. "Handicapped person" is defined in the Section 504 regulation as any person who has a physical or mental impairment which substantially limits a major life activity (*e.g.*, learning). 34 CFR § 104.3(j). Thus, depending on the severity of their condition, children with ADD may fit within that definition.

B. **Programs and Services Under Section 504**

Under Section 504, a LEA must provide a free appropriate public education to each qualified handicapped child. A free appropriate public education, under Section 504, consists of regular or special education and related aids and services that are designed to meet the individual student's needs and based on adherence to the regulatory requirements on educational setting, evaluation, placement, and procedural safeguards. 34 CFR §§ 104.33, 104.34, 104.35, and 104.36. A student may be handicapped within the meaning of Section 504, and therefore entitled to regular or special education and related aids and services under the Section 504 regulation, even though the student may not be eligible for special education and related services under Part B.

Under Section 504, if parents believe that their child is handicapped by ADD, the LEA must evaluate the child to determine whether he or she is handicapped as defined by Section 504. If a LEA determines that a child is not handicapped under Section 504, the parent has the right to contest that determination. If the child is determined to be handicapped under Section 504, the LEA must make an individualized determination of the child's educational needs for regular or special education or related aids and services. 34 CFR § 104.35. For children determined to be handicapped under Section 504, implementation of an individualized education program developed in accordance with Part B, although not required, is one means of meeting the free appropriate public education requirements of Section 504.[4] The child's education must be provided in the regular education classroom unless it is demonstrated that education in the regular environment with the use of supplementary aids and services cannot be achieved satisfactorily. 34 CFR § 104.34.

---

[4]Many LEAs use the same process for determining the needs of students under Section 504 that they use for implementing Part B.

Should it be determined that the child with ADD is handicapped for purposes of Section 504 and needs only adjustments in the regular classroom, rather than special education, those adjustments are required by Section 504. A range of strategies is available to meet the educational needs of children with ADD.

Regular classroom teachers are important in identifying the appropriate educational adaptions and interventions for many children with ADD.

SEAs and LEAs should take the necessary steps to promote coordination between special and regular education programs. Steps also should be taken to train regular education teachers and other personnel to develop their awareness about ADD and its manifestations and the adaptations that can be implemented in regular education programs to address the instructional needs of these children. Examples of adaptations in regular education programs could include the following:

> providing a structured learning environment; repeating and simplifying instructions about in-class and homework assignments; supplementing verbal instructions with visual instructions; using behavioral management techniques; adjusting class schedules; modifying test delivery; using tape recorders, computer-aided instruction, and other audio-visual equipment; selecting modified textbooks or workbooks; and tailoring homework assignments.

Other provisions range from consultation to special resources and may include reducing class size; use of one-on-one tutorials; classroom aides and note takers; involvement of a "services coordinator" to oversee implementation of special programs and services, and possible modification of nonacademic times such as lunchroom, recess, and physical education.

Through the use of appropriate adaptations and interventions in regular classes, many of which may be required by Section 504, the Department believes that LEAs will be able to effectively address the instructional needs of many children with ADD.

C. Procedural Safeguards Under Section 504

Procedural safeguards under the Section 504 regulation are stated more generally than in Part B. The Section 504 regulation requires the LEA to make available a system of procedural safeguards that permits parents to challenge actions regarding the identification, evaluation, or educational placement of their handicapped child whom they believe needs special education or related services. 34 CFR § 104.36. The Section 504 regulation requires that the system of procedural safeguards include notice, an opportunity for the parents or guardian to examine relevant records, an impartial hearing with opportunity for participation by the parents or guardian and representation by counsel, and a review procedure. Compliance with procedural safeguards of Part B is one means of fulfilling the Section 504 requirement.[5] However, in an impartial due process hearing raising issues under the Section 504 regulation, the impartial hearing officer must make a determination based upon that regulation.

V. CONCLUSION

Congress and the Department have recognized the need to provide information and assistance to teachers, administrators, parents and other interested persons regarding the identification, evaluation, and instructional needs of children with ADD. The Department has formed a work group to explore strategies across principal offices to address this issue. The work group also plans to identify some ways that the Department can work with the education associations to cooperatively consider the programs and services needed by children with ADD across special and regular education.

---

[5]Again, many LEAs and some SEAs are conserving time and resources by using the same due process procedures for resolving disputes under both laws.

In fiscal year 1991, the Congress appropriated funds for the Department to synthesize and disseminate current knowledge related to ADD. Four centers will be established in Fall, 1991 to analyze and synthesize the current research literature on ADD relating to identification, assessment, and interventions. Research syntheses will be prepared in formats suitable for educators, parents and researchers. Existing clearinghouses and networks, as well as Federal, State and local organizations will be utilized to disseminate these research syntheses to parents, educators and administrators, and other interested persons.

In addition, the Federal Resource Center will work with SEAs and the six regional resource centers authorized under the Individuals with Disabilities Education Act to identify effective identification and assessment procedures, as well as intervention strategies being implemented across the country for children with ADD. A document describing current practice will be developed and disseminated to parents, educators and administrators, and other interested persons through the regional resource centers network, as well as by parent training centers, other parent and consumer organizations, and professional organizations. Also, the Office for Civil Rights' ten regional offices stand ready to provide technical assistance to parents and educators.

It is our hope that the above information will be of assistance to your State as you plan for the needs of children with ADD who require special education and related services under Part B, as well as for the needs of the broader group of children with ADD who do not qualify for special education and related services under Part B, but for whom special education or adaptations in regular education programs are needed. If you have any questions, please contact Jean Peelen, Office for Civil Rights (Phone: 202/732-1635); Judy Schrag, Office of Special Education Programs (Phone: 202/732-1007); or Dan Bonner, Office of Elementary and Secondary Education (Phone: 202/401-0984).

U.S. DEPARTMENT OF EDUCATION
OFFICE FOR CIVIL RIGHTS
REGIONAL CIVIL RIGHTS OFFICES

REGION I—Connecticut, Maine, Massachusetts, New Hampshire, Rhode Island, Vermont

Regional Civil Rights Director
U.S. Department of Education
Office for Civil Rights, Region I
John W. McCormack Post Office and
Courthouse Building, Room 222
Boston, Massachusetts 02109-4557
(617) 223-9662   TDD (617) 223-9695

REGION II—New Jersey, New York, Puerto Rico, Virgin Islands

Regional Civil Rights Director
U.S. Department of Education
Office for Civil Rights, Region II
26 Federal Plaza, 33rd Fl, Rm. 33-130
New York, New York 10278-0082
(212) 264-4633   TDD (212) 264-9464

REGION III—Delaware, District of Columbia, Maryland, Pennsylvania, Virginia, West Virginia

Regional Civil Rights Director
U.S. Department of Education
Office for Civil Rights, Region III
3535 Market Square, Room 6300
Philadelphia, Pennsylvania 19104-3326
(215) 596-6772   TDD (215) 596-6794

REGION IV—Alabama, Florida, Georgia, Kentucky, Mississippi, North Carolina, South Carolina, Tennessee

Regional Civil Rights Director
U.S. Department of Education
Office for Civil Rights, Region IV
101 Marietta Tower-27th Floor, #2702
Mail To: P. O. Box 1705
Atlanta, Georgia 30301-1705
(404) 331-2954   TDD (404) 331-7816

REGION V—Illinois, Indiana, Minnesota, Michigan, Ohio, Wisconsin

Regional Civil Rights Director
U.S. Department of Education
Office for Civil Rights, Region V
401 South State Street-7th Fl., Suite 700C
Chicago, Illinois 60605-1202
(312) 886-3456   TDD (312) 353-2541

REGION VI—Arkansas, Louisiana, New Mexico, Oklahoma, Texas

Regional Civil Rights Director
U.S. Department of Education
Office for Civil Rights, Region VI
1200 Main Tower Building, Suite 2260
Dallas, Texas 75202-9998
(214) 767-3959   TDD (214) 767-3639

REGION VII—Iowa, Kansas, Missouri, Nebraska

Regional Civil Rights Director
U.S. Department of Education
Office for Civil Rights, Region VII
P. O. Box 901381
10220 N. Executive Hills Blvd., 8th Fl. Kansas City, Missouri 64190-1381
(816) 891-8026

REGION VIII—Colorado, Montana, North Dakota, South Dakota, Utah, Wyoming

Regional Civil Rights Director
U.S. Department of Education
Office for Civil Rights, Region VIII
1961 Stout Street, Room 342
Denver, Colorado 80294-3608
(303) 844-5695   TDD (303) 844-3417

REGION IX—Arizona, California, Hawaii, Nevada, Guam, Trust Territory of the Pacific Islands, American Samoa

Regional Civil Rights Director
U.S. Department of Education
Office for Civil Rights, Region IX
221 Main Street, 10th Floor, Suite 1020
San Francisco, California 94105-1925
(415) 227-8040   TDD (415) 227-8124

REGION X—Alaska, Idaho, Oregon, Washington

Regional Civil Rights Director
U.S. Department of Education
Office for Civil Rights, Region X
Mail Code 10-9010
915 Second Avenue, Room 3310
Seattle, Washington 98174-1099
(206) 442-1636   TDD (206) 442-4542

SUGGESTED READING AND AUDIOPROGRAMS

FOR PARENTS, TEACHERS AND PROFESSIONALS

GENERAL

Barkley, Russell, Ph.D. *Attention Deficit Hyperactivity Disorder*. New York: Guilford Press, 1990.

Copeland, Edna D. Ph.D., and Valerie L. Love, M.Ed. *Attention, Please! A Comprehensive Guide for Successfully Parenting Children with Attention Disorders and Hyperactivity (ADHD/ADD)*. Plantation, FL: Specialty Press, Inc., 1995.

Copeland, Edna D., Ph.D. *Understanding Attention Disorders: Preschool Through Adulthood*. 42 min. Atlanta: Resurgens Press, Inc., 1989. Videoprogram.

Fowler, Mary Cahill. *Maybe You Know My Kid: A Parent's Guide to Identifying, Understanding, and Helping Your Child with Attention-Deficit Hyperactivity Disorder*. New York: Carol Publishing Group, 1990.

Goldstein, Sam, Ph.D., and Michael Goldstein, Ph.D. *Managing Attention Disorders in Children: A Guide for Practitioners*. New York: John Wiley and Sons, Inc., 1990.

Ingersoll, Barbara. *Your Hyperactive Child - A Parent's Guide to Coping With Attention Deficit Disorder*. New York: Doubleday, 1988.

Kavanaugh, James, et al. (Eds.). *Learning Disabilities: Proceedings of the National Conference on Learning Disabilities*, 1987, edited by James Kavanaugh. Parkton, MD: York Press, 1988.

Stewart, M., and S. Olds. *Raising A Hyperactive Child*. New York: Harper & Row, 1975.

Taylor, John F., Ph.D. *Helping Your Hyperactive Child*. Rocklin, CA: Prima Publishing and Communications, 1990.

Weisberg, Lynne W., M.D., Ph.D., and Rosalie Greenberg, M.D. *When Acting Out Isn't Acting*. Washington: PIA Press, 1988.

Weiss, G. and L. Hechtman. *Hyperactive Children Grown Up*. New York: The Guilford Press, 1986.

MEDICATION

Copeland, Edna D., Ph.D. *Medications for Attention Disorders (ADHD/ADD) and Related Medical Problems: A Comprehensive Handbook.* Plantation, FL: Specialty Press, Inc., 1995.

Copps, Stephen C., M.D. *The Attending Physician - Attention Deficit Disorders: A Guide for Pediatricians and Family Physicians.* Plantation, FL: Specialty Press, Inc., 1992.

Silver, Larry B., M.D. *The Misunderstood Child: A Guide For Parents Of Learning Disabled Children.* New York: McGraw-Hill, 1984.

Wender, Paul H., M.D. *The Hyperactive Child, Adolescent and Adult: ADD Through The Life Span.* New York: Oxford University Press, 1987.

BEHAVIOR MANAGEMENT/RESPONSIBILITY

Barkley, Russell, Ph.D. *Defiant Children.* New York: Guilford Press, 1987.

Becker, Wesley C., Ph.D. *Parents Are Teachers.* Champaign, IL: Research Press, 1971.

Canter, Lee, and Marlene Canter. *Assertive Discipline.* New York: Harper & Row, 1985.

Copeland, Edna D., Ph.D. *Developing Your Child's Potential Through Knowledge, Discipline and Encouragement.* Confident, Capable, Cooperative Children Series, Atlanta: Resurgens Press, Inc., 1988.

Copeland, Edna D., Ph.D. *The Joy of a Job Well Done (with Responsibility Charts and a Family Organization Calendar).* Confident, Capable, Cooperative Children Series: Atlanta: Resurgens Press, Inc., 1988.

LANGUAGE/COGNITIVE THERAPY

Barkley, Russell A. *Hyperactive Children: A Handbook For Diagnosis and Treatment.* New York: Guilford Press, 1980.

Healy, Jane M., Ph.D. *Your Child's Growing Mind.* Garden City: Doubleday, 1987.

Kendall, P.C., and Braswell, L. *Cognitive-behavioral Therapy for Impulsive Children.* New York: Guilford, 1985.

ALLERGIES AND FOOD INTOLERANCES

Crook, William, M.D. *Tracking Down Hidden Food Allergy*. Jackson, TN: Professional Books, 1985.

Rapp, Doris J., M.D. *Allergies and the Hyperactive Child*. New York: Simon & Schuster, 1979.

EDUCATIONAL INTERVENTION

Anderson, Winifred, Stephen Chitwood, and Diedre Hayden. *Negotiating the Special Education Maze*. 2d ed. Rockville, MA: Woodbine House, 1990.

Copeland, Edna D., Ph.D. *Attention Disorders: The School's Vital Role*. 119 min. Atlanta: Resurgens Press, Inc., 1989. Videoprogram.

Parker, Harvey C. *The ADD Hyperactivity Workbook for Parents, Teachers and Kids*. Plantation, FL: Impact Publications, Inc., 1988.

Silver, Larry B., M.D. *The Misunderstood Child: A Guide for Parents of Learning Disabled Children*. New York: McGraw-Hill, 1984.

ADULT ADD

Barkley, Russell A. Ph.D. *Attention Deficit Hyperactivity Disorder: A Handbook for Diagnosis and Treatment*. New York: Guilford Press, 1990 (Chapter 18).

Copeland, Edna D. Ph.D., and Valerie L. Love, M.Ed. *Attention, Please! A Comprehensive Guide for Successfully Parenting Children with Attention Disorders and Hyperactivity (ADHD/ADD)*. Plantation, FL: Specialty Press, Inc., 1995 (Appendix I).

Wender, Paul H., M.D. *The Hyperactive Child, Adolescent and Adult: ADD Through the Life Span*. New York: Oxford University Press, 1987.